Thursday's
WORD

Devotional

Brenda C. Smith

Thursday's WORD

Devotional

Brenda C. Smith

inCahoots LITERARY

InCahoots
LITERARY

Published by InCahoots Literary
a division of InCahoots Film Entertainment LLC
Oklahoma City

www.incahootsliterary.com
www.incahootsfilmentertainment.com

Book design by Michael Allen of InCahoots Literary

ISBN 978-0-9887241-6-7

To my mother, Bertha Cornelia Steele Covington, who planted that small mustard seed of faith in me years ago when I was a small child attending Sunday School. She will always be my motivator, encourager, and a strong woman of faith. Mama showed me how to believe in our big God. I love you, Mama.

Contents

Acknowledgements

Thanks to my Lord and Savior Jesus Christ for trusting me with His Word to share with His people, making this book possible.

Thanks to my daughter, Quinesha, and my sons, Quinton and Quandré, who have been my constant encouragement and hope.

Thanks to my pastor Vernon Ray McGuire, Jr., and First Lady Sherrie D. McGuire of the Church of God (Sanctified) in Franklin, Tennessee. Because of their constant prayer and belief in what God has trusted me with this small book is evidence that "no good thing will he withhold from them who walk uprightly." My Thursday's Word group who are all gems in my life.

A very special thank you to the late Bishop Andrew John Valentine, Jr. who has been my spiritual leader and supporter down through the years. Thank you Sir, for all you've done in helping to develop my gifts that I will use in the Kingdom of God.

Thanks to my spiritual prayer warriors: Sisters Barbara Hughes, Evelyn Hickerson, Thelma Walden, Mother Juanita Hamilton, and Evangelist Claudine Black. Without the fervent prayers of these wailing women this book would still be a dream. My church family on Green Street were all instrumental in this small treasure. I thank you.

Thank you to Denise Thomas, Katherine Covington Shelton, Delilah Varnum, and Doretha Walker for being believers in me and God's gift He planted on the inside of me.

Yes, Doretha… "I CAN FLY."

Thursday's
WORD
Devotional

Brenda C. Smith

Jesus says that it only takes a mustard seed amount of faith (confidence) in the Word of God to do the impossible.

Brenda C. Smith

"And Jesus said unto them, "Because of your unbelief: for verily I say unto you, If ye have faith as a grain of mustard seed, ye shall say unto this mountain, Remove hence to yonder place; and it shall remove; and nothing shall be impossible unto you."" – Matthew 17:20 (KJV)

Thursday's Word

God has given us many gifts. Of all the gifts that he gave - He is the greatest! He gave us himself. As believers of Jesus Christ, you and I are containers of God. We hold him within the fragile clay jars of our bodies. The Apostle Paul explained it this way: "For God, who said, "Let there be light in darkness," has made us understand that this light is the brightness of the glory of God that is seen in the face of Jesus Christ." A container is an object used for or capable of holding, especially for transporting or storage.

King David said in Psalm 119:11, *"Thy Word have I hid in mine heart, that I might not sin against thee."* David knew where to keep the Word so it would not be easily taken from him. He knew that the Word needed to be in his heart because that is where our Lord lives when He is inside of us. He also stated in Psalm 51:10, *"Create in me a clean heart, O God; and renew a right spirit in me."* We are the containers that God has chosen to carry His Word, His Light, His Wisdom, and His Ways. We are traveling from one place to another so we need to keep our lives as uncomplicated as possible. We are transporters of and storage containers of all that is good in Him. A sinner in the world should not have to take a microscope, a telephoto lens, or a magnifying glass to be able to see Jesus in you! You should light up the room upon entering. Every head should turn because something has happened in the atmosphere. A shift has occurred. You are not bringing yourself into the room, but you are carrying Jesus on the inside of you. *"But this precious treasure – this light and power that now shine within us – is held in perishable containers, that is, in our weak bodies. So everyone can see that our glorious power is from God and is not our own."* – 2 Corinthians 4:6–7 (NLT).

When people are hurting, they look around for comfort. They feel they cannot bring Jesus down to them. Some of us still think of God as being far, far away (and He is in heaven). But, he is as close as your heartbeat and your breath that you breathe. We call on Jesus in our distress, and He truly hears us. He answers by sending someone to hold our hands. He sends someone who can talk with us. He sends others who pray with us. All those good things that you do you are making Jesus real in the eyes of the ones in need. You have become His hands and feet, by loving others, and helping them through their problems. I love this quote from Kay Warren, "We are God with 'skin' on. We make Him personal and intimate."

Know today, that God loves you, and He wants you to be happy, peaceful and full of His joy.

May God continue to bless you is my prayer in Jesus' Name.

Our Thoughts

Thought: the act or process of thinking, reasoning and imagining. Negative: expressing or containing negation or denial.

Did you know that the average person has 10,000 separate thoughts each day? Everyone of those thoughts represents a choice you make, a decision to think about this, and not about that. Norman Vincent Peale said, "Change your thoughts, and you change the world." Henry Ford gave that truth a different spin when he declared, "Thinking is the hardest work in the world, which is probably why so few people engage in it." There have been many sermons, lectures, speeches, or papers written on "thoughts" and "thinking." Why? Because your thoughts really do matter in how you choose to live your life. So many people struggle with negative thinking. Negative thoughts poison the mind, and ultimately the soul. Believers are told to "take every thought captive" that doesn't conform to Christ's standards. We must evaluate everyone of our actions, desires, and impulses, and bring everything under the control of Jesus (2 Cor 10:5).

Here are four examples of negative thinking:

Self-Pity: We all fall into this trap sooner or later. As the saying goes, "Into each life some rain must fall." We sometimes feel we have been dealt an unfair hand, while others are basking in the sunshine.

Blaming: This is an attempt to find a scapegoat for your problems. You can't face things on your own, so you find another person who seems to be the source of your problems.

Unwillingness to Change: You are a victim and the world is against you. Since, you can't change, then, your behavior can't be your own fault. So you never have to face it honestly. "I have every right to be hurt, and I'm not going to give it up."

Anger and Bitterness: You refuse to accept the fact that you yourself are the source of your own problems. When others suggest otherwise, you get angry, defensive and bitter. You remember every miserable thing ever done to you or against you.

YOUR THOUGHTS MATTER! NEGATIVE THINKING LEADS TO NEGATIVE LIVING.

"Finally, brothers, whatever is true, whatever is noble, whatever is right, whatever is pure, whatever is lovely, whatever is admirable – if anything is excellent or praiseworthy – think about such things." – Philippians 4:8.

Wisdom and Knowledge

The accumulation of so much information has caused many to believe that 21st century man is the wisest creature to have ever lived. This belief has fostered the created arrogance and pride among educators and the educated in the world. It has caused man to believe he no longer needs God. Therefore, man is serving the created world rather than the Creator of the world. He is looking at all his mess, and he cannot hear from the Messenger. He has created so much chaos that he can't find peace. He is confused, misinformed, frustrated, suffering from poor judgment, and spiraling out of control. *"Because of that, when they knew God, they glorified him not as God, neither were thankful; but became vain in their imaginations, and their foolish heart was darkened. Professing themselves to be wise, they became fools."* – Romans 1:21. Today, our problem is that man's knowledge has surpassed his wisdom. Our world needs the true wisdom that comes from God, and whoever wills may come to Him, through Jesus Christ and freely receive Heavenly Divine wisdom. Knowledge is the accumulation of facts. Wisdom is the ability to use facts responsibly.

Everyone will not achieve an "ivy league" education. Nor will everyone achieve great success in science, math, aerospace, or in a professional world. But, everyone can have the wisdom of God. "The fear of the Lord is the beginning of Wisdom; a good understanding have all those who do His commandments. His praise endures forever." – Psalm 111:10. Understanding is a critical aspect relating directly to knowledge and wisdom. Understanding is a step beyond knowledge. It is the ability to evaluate the knowledge.

This requires seeing the big picture, to see how the knowledge fits. To understand knowledge is to see the meaning or significance of the knowledge. Yet, this is not wisdom? Wisdom has less to do with knowledge than it has to do with the application of knowledge in a very specific way. Many of our professional athletes are considered pros. Because of their ability they can play their sport on a higher level of skill than you and I can. They have skillsets they use to the highest caliber of playing the game in order to win championships and Superbowls. They are not playing to be playing – they are playing to win!

Likewise, we should pursue wisdom to win in life. Wisdom is that quality that enables one to live a noticeably, recognizably outstanding life. Only God understands the way to wisdom, because he alone is the source of true wisdom. The wisdom of God is evident in the beauty, richness, intricacy, variety and splendor of the created order, and is also evident in the person, powers and perfections of God of creation. To fear God is to nurture an attitude of awe and humility before him and to walk in radical dependence upon God in each area of life.

We are given the opportunity to learn wisdom from others who are further down the road than we are. We don't have to live and learn; we can learn and live.

What Is Faith?

Faith is defined in the first verse of chapter of the Bible, Hebrews 11, *"Now faith is the substance of things hoped for, the evidence of things not seen."* It means persuasion, conviction of religious truth, conviction of the truthfulness of God, or reliance on God. This verse tells us that faith is assurance that we will receive the things for which we hope, and it supports the knowledge that we will receive them. The Bible has promises for blessings in this life if we obey God, and it also contains promises for eternal life in the kingdom of God. Faith is the assurance that we will receive those promises.

Faith is also the evidence of proof of what we cannot see or what we have not seen yet. By faith we know that God made the universe, although we cannot see God and were not present at the creation. Faith is the evidence or proof that God exists, and it is also the evidence that He will keep His promises, even though we have not seen those promises yet.

This verse does define faith in terms of the five senses: sight, hearing, touch, smell, and taste. If we could perceive the object of our faith, we would not need faith.

Romans 4:16–21 describes the relationship that the Old Testament patriarch Abraham had with God: *"being fully convinced that what He had promised He was also able to perform."* Abraham had faith that God could keep His promises, and he was assured that he would receive them. He had the evidence, which is faith.

Let us consider what faith is not. Faith is not merely believing in Christ, John 8:31, *"Then said Jesus to those Jews which believed on him, If ye continue in my word, then are ye my disciples indeed."* They believed in Christ, but did not believe His message.

How Do We Receive Faith? *"For by grace you have been saved through faith, and that not of yourselves; it is the gift of God."* – Ephesians 2:5. We are to live by Christ's faith in us, his gift to us.

Faith is a part of the fruit of God's Holy Spirit. Galatians 5:22–23 – *"But the fruit of the Spirit is love, joy, peace, longsuffering, gentleness, goodness, faith, meekness, temperance: against such there is no law."*

God may not answer our prayers immediately, if He did we would not need faith for very long. He may not come when we want Him, but He is always on time. If we have faith, we know that God is able to work miracles in our lives, that He can protect us physically and heal us. He will provide for our needs, and often He will even provide for our wants. Most importantly, by faith He will develop His holy, righteous character in us in order that we can become members of His family.

Hebrews 10:34–38 states, *"The just shall live by faith."* The Bible is full of promises for this life and for eternal life in the kingdom of God. God is looking for people who believe. Are you a believer in Jesus Christ?

Condemnation

Condemnation: to Blame or Sentence. To Declare Something Is Unfit to Live In.

How many times today have you allowed Satan to condemn you? How many times have you allowed him to whisper in your ear that you are not worthy of God's love? One time is too many for a child of God!

Condemnation comes from Satan (automatically, it's no good) and is meant to tear you down. It will point out your failures and how badly you've messed up. Shows you the problem - but where's the solution?

"God did not send His Son into the world to condemn the world, but that the world through Him might be saved." – John 3:17. The purpose of Jesus coming into the world was to save it. He did not condemn the world because the world, the people in it, were already condemned. John 3:18 reads, *"He who believes in him is not condemned; but he who does not believe is condemned already, because he has not believed in the name of the only begotten son of God."* Nobody is born into this world as a believer in Jesus Christ, therefore, we are all condemned to an eternity separated from God because we are born spiritually dead to Him in our sins. Jesus did not need to come into the world to condemn us because we were already condemned; dead to God in sin.

However, Jesus came into the world to save us by dying for our sins which originally caused God to remove His life from us, in Adam, back in the Garden of Eden (Genesis 2:7, 17). Therefore, since the death of Jesus Christ dealt with the sin problem for all eternity, He could then offer the life of God, lost in Adam, back to us as a free gift. So, if you believe in Jesus you, have become born again of the Spirit of God; made alive to God. And because of the Cross there is no sin that can now cause God to remove His life from you. That is why life is an eternal life; a life that carries you through your physical life, past death and on into eternity. You are now saved. Saved from the wages of sin, death, by the gift of God, life in Jesus (Romans 6:23). You are no longer condemned with those in the world who do not believe in Jesus Christ (Romans 8:1).

This is what you say because of the Accusing Spirit of Satan:

You say, "But Satan keeps bringing it up." That's because he is called the "accuser" (Revelation 12:10). But notice how you overcome Satan the accuser: *"They overcame him by the blood of the Lamb, and by the word of their testimony;"* – Revelation 12:11.

You remark, "But, I don't feel forgiven." Forgiveness comes by faith, not feelings. As long as you live by feelings Satan has a weapon he can use against you at every turn.

Next time Satan accuses you, exclaim, "I'm glad you brought that up." Then tell him what the blood of Jesus has accomplished on your behalf. If you do that, he will flee.

How do we combat this deceitful spirit? Fill our mind with the voice of God. Read and study His Word.

If You Make That Bed Hard, You Will Have to Lay on It!

Pillow: a rectangular cloth bag stuffed with feathers, foam, rubber, or other soft materials used to support the head when lying down or sleeping.

Pillar: a tall vertical structure of stone, wood, or metal, used as a support for a building, or as an ornament or monument.

That is an old saying that I use to hear a lot growing up. I think that describes a lot of what we are going through right today. It is because we are sleeping on beds that we made ourselves. Some have made beds that are soft, fluffy, and feathery – easy to sleep on. You are blessed with having good dreams. Others have made the mistake of making their beds hard – rough, tough, pins, needles, and knives in them. Nightmares are made when we sleep on hard beds. We chose these beds by the choices we made early in life. Some came about because we felt we knew it all and did not have to listen to the advice of the wise men and women who had "been there" and "done that." I wanted to believe that will not happen to me because I am wiser than all of them giving me advice, although, you were barely eighteen or twenty-one at the time.

This reminds me of Jacob in the Bible. Jacob needed salvation. He was surrounded by people who loved him and would willingly save him, but they were not able to do so. Salvation is an individual need and an individual experience. Jacob needed to know God for himself. He was taken to a hard place in Genesis 28:10–12, *"And he lighted upon a certain place, and tarried there all night, because the sun was set; and he took of the stones of that place, and put them for his pillows, and lay down in that place to sleep. And he dreamed, and behold a ladder set up on the earth, and the top of it reached to heaven: and behold the angels of God ascending and descending on it."* The ladder that Jacob saw was no other than Jesus Christ himself! Jesus is the way you get to heaven. He can be that bridge that you need to cross over your troubled waters. *"For there is one God, and one meditator between God and men, the man Christ Jesus."* – I Timothy 2:25.

Just as surely as you fall asleep each night upon your pillow, God is needing to use that pillow and turn it into a pillar of faith. The God of a hard place will show up just for you! Jacob was in a dark place, a hard place, a confused place, he was tired, and it was night time. His pillow became a pillar of faith because he learned that Jesus was the rock. You can rest on the rock of Jesus Christ, because He is the Rock of your Salvation.

Disappoint – Discourge

Disappoint: to let down. To not turn out as expected.

Discourge: to deprive of courage, hope and confidence.

The raise doesn't happen. The promotion is given to someone else. The promise isn't kept. Being let down is a part of the human experience. It isn't an easy part of it. It is especially hard when we think we have been misled or lied to in some way. When we get our hopes up, then, we face the crushing feeling of seeing them smashed. Disappointment is hard to deal with.

The boss was dishonest. The friend didn't keep your confidence. They can leave us in despair. It is in times of disappointment, when we are convinced that no one can be trusted, that the faithfulness of God is truly seen. In Scripture the phase "I will never leave you or forsake you" is used on several occasions. It is a reminder that no matter the situation God is there. He is faithful. He will NOT disappoint. When others let you down, don't give in, because God is still there. He is faithful.

The best way to handle any disappointment is to express it to God. He already knows how you feel and why. But pouring your heart out to him prepares you to experience His love and comfort. Remind yourself that God is still in control, and he has the highest good in mind for you. *"Thy way, O God, is in the sanctuary: who is so great a God as our God? Thou are the God that doest wonders: thou hast declared thy strength among the people."* – Psalm 77:13–14.

It was advertised that the devil was going to put his tools up for sale. On the date of the sale the tools were placed for public inspection, each being marked with its sale price. There were a treacherous lot of implements: hatred, envy, jealous, doubt, lying, and pride. Laid apart from the rest of the pile was a harmless-looking tool, well-worn and priced very high.

"What's the name of the tool?" asked one of the purchasers.
"Oh? said the adversary, "That's Discouragement?
"Why have you priced it so high?"

"Because it's more useful to me than the others. I can pry open and get inside a person's heart with that one, when I cannot get near him with other tools. Now once I get inside, I can make him do what I choose. It's a badly worn tool, because I use it on almost everyone since few people know it belongs to me?"

The devil's price for Discouragement was so high, he never sold it. It's still his major tool, and he still uses it on God's people today. So, God has to come along and remind us of all the promises he made to us. All the things He's already done. Memory is a good thing when you remember the right things. The devil can only remind you of your past to keep you from enjoying your present. As a Christian, he is not part of your future!

It's Time We Got Disturbed

We often think of disturbance as annoyances. Please don't disturb me. I need to be alone. Knock before entering. Close the door when you leave. Disturbance means to interrupt the quiet, rest, peace, or order. It means to interfere with or hinder. I know these can be issues for some, but please I want you to also understand that some disturbances can be healthy or given as a "wake up call" to put you back (if you have fallen) on the right track. It is easy to get onto the wrong track in life, and it can be quite unsettling until we get back running smoothly again. In referencing the recent tornadoes that touched down in this area, there is a need to be disturbed when you have 70 degree weather and rising temperatures in the cold of January. Yes, there is nothing we can personally do about the weather, but we can take notice and know that when there is an alert or siren sounding to take cover in your "safe place" in your homes. Ignoring the warning can be dangerous. As our bodies age, let us be disturbed when things start to happen, blood pressure rises, can't sleep well, weight gain, or unexplained weight loss. Not to panic, but to be disturbed enough to go seek help from your doctor.

I believe we have become complacent and comfortable where we are now. We are just muddling through without a care for others in this world. As long as no one disturbs us we are fine. We are content, and we are happy. Well, saints, Jesus comforts the disturbed and disturbs the comfortable. Nature is speaking to us and telling us that God is bringing about a shift. He needs for us to rise up and accept the challenges of teaching, preaching, evangelizing, praying, and giving in a whole new way! We have a whole new generation of people that do not know Jesus Christ. They need to get saved, baptized, and ready to work alongside us in kingdom building. I am not speaking of anyone being "mentally disturbed" that you set out to do a BAD thing. I am speaking to people who are "disturbed mentally" that they are willing to go out and try to make a difference in the lives of others – to offer Godly counsel to those in need, to help a child learn to read, to go visit the elderly, and to offer prayer for the healing of strife in your families.

I believe that God is looking for some disturbed people. He is searching for men and women, students, and young adults who will allow Him to disturb them by making them truly see the world in which we live – so disturbed that they will be compelled to do something about what they see. If we do not become disturbed by the world in which we live, we will be consumed with the trivial, the insignificant, and the temporary. We do not want to be in danger of living by the wrong measurement of success, evaluating our legacy by the wrong standard. Jesus Christ is our standard.

Jesus' words *"Much is required from those to whom much is given."* – Luke 12:48 (NLT). Disturbances should be taking place in your minds, taking root in your soul, and one day take you on a journey to want to help and heal others.

Judge Not

Judge: a public officer authorized to hear and decide cases in a court of law; a magistrate charged with the administration of justice.

Judge ye not! If you see someone who is stumbling, do you think he is drunk? If you see someone who is dirty, do you think he is homeless? If you see someone who is asking for money, do you assume he is a beggar? If we are passing judgment, we are not qualified. From the very definition we are not qualified. We don't know enough about the person to judge him. We don't know enough about his past. We condemn a man for stumbling this morning, but we didn't see the blows he took on yesterday. We judge a person who is asking for money, yet we don't know who he had to feed on last night. We see a man who is dirty, but we don't know if he had to walk around dirty for his children to be clean. Perhaps, they fell the last time they got up. I see them rising above it all. I see them prosperous. I see them saved and filled with the Holy Ghost. They are our assignments. The saved do not need us. We are to help those who are lost. *"For the Son of man is come to save that which was lost."* – Matthew 18:11. We were lost at one time, too. Thank God He sent His only begotten Son to save us. Dare we judge a book while chapters are yet unwritten? Should we pass a verdict on a painting while the artist still holds the brush?

There is a righteous kind of Judgment we are supposed to exercise with careful discernment (John 7:24). When Jesus told us not to judge (Matthew 7:1), He was telling us not to judge hypocritically. *"For in the same way you judge others, you will be judged, and with the measure you use, It will be measured to you. Why do you look at the speck of sawdust in your brother's eye and pay no attention to the plank in your own eye? How can you say to your brother, 'Let me take the speck out of your eye, and then you will see clearly to remove the speck from your brother's eye.'"* What Jesus was condemning here was hypocritical, self-righteous judgment of others. Don't judge someone else for their sin when you are sinning even worse. If a believer sees another believer sinning, it is his Christian duty to lovingly and respectfully confront the person with his sin (Matthew 18:15–17). This is not judging, but rather pointing out the truth in hope and with the ultimate goal of bringing repentance in the other person and restoration to fellowship. We are to speak the truth in love (Ephesians 4:15).

Rest

Rest: to be calm. Not to deal with the problem anymore.

How many times have you wanted to give up on something or someone? You instead cried out to God and he helped you. If you are an individual who fixes everything, this is not easy. As soon as one problem is dealt with another one comes along. I fixed the hole in the bucket, and before long another one springs up and water is leaking again. You know the scenario. Sometimes, we just want problems to go away. But remember what Jesus said in John 16:33, *"In this world you will have trouble. But take heart! I have overcame the world."* There is no question that we all have problems from time to time. Many times we dig a hole and expect God to fill it up for us. Most often we are trying to find peace through what the world has to offer rather than what God, in Christ, has already offered to us, and then are deflated when it does not happen. There is nothing in the world that is designed to offer us the peace that only comes from resting in Christ and His finished work.

We can even compare the problems we have to rain coming down, streams rising and winds beating against a house. We are God's "house," the temple of the Holy Spirit, the Body of Christ. That doesn't mean that we are immune to problems in this world. The scriptures tell us that God will be with us before, during and after we experience these struggles and keep us from falling. The only way to cope with our struggles is to get in the Word of God. We need to believe in His promises. The Bible says, *"The thief comes only to steal and kill and destroy; I have come that they may have life, and have it to the full."* – John 10:10.

It is Satan, with his lies and deception, that is able to mislead Christians into believing that the trials of life are something strange and not to be experienced by a believer. The pressures of life only reveal the validity of what we say we believe. If when these pressures arrive in our life and we are left without the ability to rest, it may be due to the fact that we are trying to live the Christian life in the energy of our own flesh. *"To this end I labor, struggling with all his energy, which so powerfully works in me."* – Colossians 1:29. We cannot live the Christian life without Christ! Jesus Christ was the only one that ever did live it and now, through the indwelling of the Holy Spirit, wants to live His life through us. God wants us to rest and has promised us that rest in Christ. He did for us what we could not do for ourselves. We rest because we know that God will use these troubles, struggles, and circumstances for our good.

We rest from trying to gain or maintain our right-standing before God through our own efforts. God has blessed us with every spiritual blessing (Ephesians 1:3). So while the devil may try and use our circumstances to rob us of the joy of our salvation, we can rest assured that what we experience is not indicative of who we are in God's sight and what we have in His Son.

Cling

Cling: to hold tight, as by grasping or embracing; cleave.

Do you remember as a child when you would cling to your dad or mom when you felt danger approaching? *"My soul followeth hard after thee; thy right hand upholdeth me."* – Psalm 63:8. The words "followeth hard" have the idea of clinging unto the Lord. When danger, temptations and sorrows approach, the best response is to cling to Our Heavenly Father. He alone can carry us through the tough times. The world in which we live in is a dangerous place. We are facing temptations from Satan, the lusts of our own flesh, and pressures from the world to conform. Because of these dangers, we need to cling to our Lord each step of the way. When we let go of the Lord, we not only find ourselves being exposed to dangers from without, but also the dangers from within our hearts.

Dependence: Without God we cannot face the dangers or pitfalls that lie ahead of us. The storms in our lives make us depend on God. He will see us safely through each one. King David battled Goliath totally depending upon the Lord. Like David, no matter how big the danger before us, we cling to God's Word to give us the victory.

Declare Your Love: Have you left your first love? Like the church at Ephesus did? When this happens, you are allowing your love to grow cold toward the Lord. You are not attending church or participating in worship to him. You are not reading and studying His Word. This lack of love creates greater opportunities to fall into temptations, to doubt God's love and provision, and to live a selfish life before others.

Dare to Move: Loving God means we need to stay as close to Him as possible. We want to enjoy our time of communion with him. We want to listen to the Word of God. We are not ashamed, but we are proud to cling to our Savior and our Lord.

CLINGING: like a vine clings to life on the true vine of Jesus Christ.

To Cut with Scissors or Shears

How many of you have gone to the beauty shop or barber shop and gotten your hair cut? But, you asked for a clip. To a barber you may say, "I just want a little off the top." To a beautician you may say, "Just clip the split ends." That may be most of your head of hair that is damaged by split ends. For some reason they don't hear the word "clip." I believe they are trained to cut, and that is what they do most of the time. But, I am still on the subject of birds. Don't know why, but we have another story about a bird today.

Clipped wings could be contributing to why this bird is not desiring to come out of his cage. Clipped wings may have caused painful falls in the past. We fall down, but we get up! Also the ability to fly increases the bird's confidence. If the bird wings are currently clipped, you will have to allow it time to grow out. If the bird can't fly, he will have to spend a lot of time walking on the ground. Thus, increasing his chances of been eaten, being injured, or even killed. Many of us are walking around with clipped wings. We have been hurt. We have been set aside. We have been placed in cages of despair, anger, anguish, and even tormenting ourselves. We allow other people to place us in these cages. To prevent us from growing to our full potential, they will clip our wings.

When Jesus sees us in cages, he comes along and spends quality time with us on a daily basis. He will make us feel safe and trusting towards Him. He will sit next to the cage with the door open and talk calmly with us. He will offer us food to eat and water to drink. Every now and then he will offer us treats from His hands. He will allow us to eat from His hand. That is a truly trusting bird who allows you to feed him from your hands! The true gift comes when Jesus will allow you, little bird, to one day sing this wonderful song, "His Eye Is on the Sparrow."

"Look at the birds of the air, for they neither sow nor reap nor gather into barns; yet your heavenly Father feeds them. Are you not of more value than they?" – Matthew 6:26. Let us close with this, *"Are not two sparrows sold for a copper coin? And not one of them falls to the ground apart from your Father's will."* [30] *"But the very hairs of your head are all numbered."* [31] *"Do not fear therefore; you are of more value than many sparrows."* – Matthew 10:29–31. The bird's natural instinct to forage and interact with the world will win out over the fear. Don't worry, God's got it.

Double Portion

Double: twice as large. Two fold in size.

Portion: The part of an estate that goes to an heir.

Isaiah 61:6–7 – "And you will be called priests of the Lord. You will feed on the wealth of nations, and in their riches you will boast. Instead of their shame My people will receive a double portion. They will inherit a double portion in their land."

God wants to bless His people. He wants to demonstrate His love and kindness through His blessings bestowed upon His people. Jesus came that he might open up the blessing of God to those who believe. God is not stingy with His blessings, but He gives more than what is needed.

We have walked through some barren places in our lives. We have been disappointed, frustrated, sick, felt helpless, and even tired. We have looked to others for help and found none. We have asked for assistance, and it had run out. Everyone is in need of a double portion blessing. Before we can take hold of these blessings we need to start our journey:

1. A Journey of Faith (Bethel). Bethel is a place of hearing and believing. God wants you to be able to hear and believe that which he is telling you. God is speaking to your heart to do the impossible. The double portion is the life of Christ and the power of the Holy Spirit abiding in you. Abraham heard from God in Bethel;

he moved, pitched a tent, and built an altar. God is saying to you, "I am going to bless you. I am going to multiply you. I am going to bless the world through you." Worship God in the tent where you are. Are you in Bethel?

2. A Journey of Trust (Jericho). Jericho is the place of conquering worship. It is a place of quietness and confidence in God. It's where the man says, "I've heard His Word and I believe God" It was in Jericho that Joshua met Christ himself and took off his shoes (Joshua 5). It is a place where human plans die and faith in God begins to take over. It was in Jericho where the seven priests bearing seven trumpets and rams' horns before the ark of the Lord went before the people. They marched around and around the city that was impossible to conquer in the natural. God supernaturally stepped in and the walls felled down. Are you in Jericho?

All the while, they were praising and worshiping our Lord. Be quiet, and blow your trumpet! Say nothing! God has spoken, and nothing needs to be said. Start trusting God that everything he said is true. He is not a man that he should lie, and when he speaks, he will do what he says he will do.

The Scars May Show

The scars may show
But the pain is gone
I bore this pain, but not alone
I had to go through hell
To receive my healing
The scar may show, but it has no feeling.

The pain was heavy
It almost broke my spirit
I went through hell
To receive my healing
I know the scar is visible
But it has no feeling.

The scar may be ugly
My surgeon had to go in deep
It was all removed and I have no time to weep
I'm no longer in hell
I claimed my healing
The scar may show
But, it has no feeling.

The scars of life may show
But it will be the healing you'll know
For Jesus bathed your soul with healing
You may see the scar
But, it has no feeling.

The Church That Is Alive
and Worth the Drive

A small church nestled in a historic town
Not far from the square, five points, is where we're found
You can't see it from a distance for we have no steeple
Our light is illuminated by the love of God's people
Located in the section called "hard bargain"
For they wrestled and tugged over money for the land
And the Church of God (Sanctified) is where we stand.

We believe in Jesus and baptizing of the Holy Ghost
Like David we greet you with the Lord of hosts
We praise our Savior with hands lifted in the air
We enter in the door and leave our worldly cares
With faith we abide and our church door is ajar
To welcome all our guests who traveled near and far.

Living water refreshes you like from Jacob's well
Once you're in God's presence you cannot help but tell
Witness to others of the church along the way
But, if you're not careful you'll be back to stay!
We believe in giving our all to a God that is alive
And you will see that worshipping with us was worth the drive.

We allow you to worship freely, praising God in the way you feel
Pastor's preaching is anointed with the Holy Spirit's zeal
The choir is singing, clapping their hands, and tambourine

Whatever your instrument we encourage all to join in and sing
We are not ashamed of the gospel of Jesus Christ
For with his blood he paid the sacrifice.

Stop your searching for a church to fit your life
Come listen to the word of God and release some of your strife
We are a small church that is growing by leaps and bounds
And praising our Savior is where we want to be found
We are building God's kingdom – come don't be left out
When Gabriel blows his horn there will be no time to shout.

Come in get acquainted with a church that is alive
And you will leave assured it was worth the drive!

A Witness to Healing

Have you ever witnessed a healing?
Or taken part in someone's restoration
Have you seen without a doubt?
A person healed from the inside out

A friend of mine was sick
And I stopped by her office one day
But before I got ready to leave
She asked me if I'd pray

She had faith enough to ask
And hope enough to believe
That our prayers would be answered
And her healing she'd receive

Through Libby's faith in Jesus
And her trust in his saving power
Showed me how she depends
On his strength every hour

To be used as an instrument
To give him glory
For when Libby was healed
I, too, have a story

To spread the word that miracles
Are happening still
And all we need to do is
Pray and ask the Savior to do his will

What Is Prayer?

Praying is like talking to your best friend! It is your open and direct communication with God. He wants us to communicate with Him, like a person-to-person phone call. Cell phones and other devices have become a necessity to some people in today's society. We have Bluetooth devices, Blackberries, and talking computers. These means of communication that allow two or more people to interact, discuss, and respond to one another.

To many people prayer seems complicated, bothersome, and tiring. They think they have to have a broad scope of the English language to communicate to God, so He will understand them. Jesus is our example when it comes to prayer. He prayed for those who would come to believe in Him through the Gospel message (John 17).

Pray with faith. It is impossible to please God without faith Hebrews 11:6 – *"Anyone who wants to come to him must believe that there is a God and that he rewards those who diligently seek him."*

Pray with worship and reverence. *"Exalt the Lord our God! Bow low before his feet, for he is holy!"* – Psalm 99:5. Pray knowing that no matter how far you roam, your connection with him can never be lost.

Prayer is a place where pride is abandoned, hope is lifted, and supplication is made. Prayer is the place of admitting our need, or adopting humility, and claiming dependence on God. Prayer is the needed practice of all Christians. You pray consistently, trusting God. You pray for others, trusting God. You pray because God hears us.

Prayer changes the one praying because in prayer, you are in the presence of God as you lay before Him your complete self in confession and dependence. *"Draw near to God and he will draw near to you."* – James 4:8. One great benefit to prayer is Peace. *"Be anxious for nothing, but in everything by prayer and supplication with thanksgiving let your requests be made known to God. And the peace of God, which surpasses all comprehension, shall guard your heart and your minds in Christ Jesus."* – Philippians 4:6–7.

There is nothing in this world like the peace of God. When you are able to sit down with your family, friends and co-workers and be at peace with the things in your life, it is supreme! God wants us to have peace in our lives. He is Jehovah Shalom, the God of Peace. Peace is with God and in God. Allow His peace to fill your hearts today.

Examples of prayer in the Bible: Luke 18:1, Romans 12:12, Ephesians 6:18. God's house is to be a house of prayer (Mark 11:17). And God's people are to be people of prayer (Jude 1:20–21).

Prayer That Takes Flight –
Is One That's Prayed Right

When you say your prayers at night
Are you concerned you're praying right?
Are you checking every line?
To ensure you're not wasting time.

Are all the lines rehearsed?
Did you leave out a quote or a favorite verse?
Are you shifting on your knees?
Trying hard with God to please.

Then your prayer cannot take flight.
Because you are not praying it right.

Talk to God the way you would a friend
Don't try to impress Him with words you don't comprehend
Give him honor and acknowlege Him as king
Thank him for all the things he did bring.

Do not get locked into a particular format
You do not have to kneel, bow or even use a mat
No need to be in a certain place
In order to stand in the presence of God's face.

Take time out of each day
Ask Jesus to show you how to pray
You prayer life has to be made strong
You can even pray to Him in a song.

There's no method better than another
Just be sure to pray for your sisters and brothers
Lift up the names of the sick and wounded souls
Pray for God's love to make all of them whole.

Be patient and take time to care
Because Jesus he's always there
No appointments has to be made
No money is needed – he cannot be paid.

Praying

It's praying time. Saints, there should never be a time in your life that you are not praying – prayers of thanksgiving, gratitude, encouragement, praying for the sick, and for yourself. Always a reason, but praying is more than asking God for things. It is simply a way to commmunicate with God. Remember this: God has planned for us much more than we even dare to imagine.

PRAYER FOR STRENGTH (for yourself or someone in need): Lord, you are Holy above all others, and all the strength that I need is in your hands. I am not asking, Lord, that you take this trial away. Instead, I simply ask that You give me the strength to get through it. I will admit that it is hard, Lord. Sometimes, I feel like I can't go on. The pain and the feeling of hopelessness can be great. Philippians 4:13 states, *"I can do all things through Christ who strengthens me."* Lord, I am trusting in Your Word in Jesus name. Amen.

At times it can feel like the world is weighing down on your shoulders and that your life is falling apart. Sometimes you have no control over what is going on in your life. You just can't seem to make things better. No matter what it is that your going through or how big your obstacles are even if they are as big as mountains, all you have to do is pray for strength. Just say, "God, I pray for strength. Please give me the strength and courage that I need to win this battle. I can't do it alone." Then continue to personalize your prayer to fit your current situation. Our God is a God of miracles. No matter how bad you think it is, God can make it better.

"But when you pray, use not vain repetitions, as the heathen [do]: for they think they shall be heard for their much speakins-" – Matthew 6:1.

"And whatsoever ye shall say in my name, that will I do, that the Father may be glorified in the Son." – John 14:13.

As you pray, await your answer to your prayers. God will answer you and give you the wisdom and revelation you need mostly through scripture. You can pray alone, or find a prayer partner or a prayer group. All of this is to strengthen you and make you stronger in the Lord.

Medley to Jesus

Oh taste and see how sweet
When at Jesus' feet I'll meet
Amazing Grace how sweet the sound
To hear Jesus' voice all around.

I came to Jesus "Just As I Am"
I've lived my life to see the Lamb
Mine eyes have seen the glory
Living for Jesus gives me a story.

For God so loved the world he gave his only son
Showers of blessings I praise Him for everyone
What a friend – what a friend
And on him my life depends.

Pass me not, Oh gentle Savior
It's in you I want to find favor
I want to live in my mansion in the sky
When I bid this old world good-bye.

Just a closer walk with thee
Grant it Lord is my plea
There's a bright side somewhere
To live with Jesus without a care.

Oh I want to see Him look upon his face
To see the one who saved me by his grace
Hide me behind the mountain
Fill me with the blood from the fountain.

When you've done all you can do stand
Jesus will reach down to take your hand
Soon and very soon we are going to see the king
To savor all that heaven has to bring.

Shepherd's Joy

Shepherds watched sheep on a hill afar
When suddenly light engulfed them from a star
It's illumination was so bright
It lit up the whole dark night.

They became frightened and wanted to hide
But the angel spoke and put their fears aside
For what I have to tell will bring you great joy
Your Savior has been born-a beautiful boy.

The shepherds soon left their sheep
They set out on a journey no time to sleep
For looking for their Savior caused confusion
They had to prove this was no illusion.

So off to Bethleham the shepherds went
They needed a gift, but no money was spent
A present was given in the form of a lamb
And Jesus grew up to be called, "The great I am."

When they found my Savior in the stable that night
It was a revelation – a glorious sight
They bowed down with praise and lifted their hands
Our Savior was born to save these lands.

The gift they gave may have been small
The shepherds gave their best – it was their all
They ran throughout Bethleham telling the story
Our Savior is born. Praise God in glory!

Work

Work: effort directed to produce or accomplish something.

"Faith without works is dead." – James 2:20.

Are you giving life to your faith? If we aren't doing something that shows we believe God, the Bible says that our faith is dead. Dead faith won't accomplish anything. We have to give life to our faith by putting actions behind it. It doesn't have to be anything big, just something that shows your faith in God. For example, I know people who are down and discouraged. They pray, "God, please get me out of this discouragement. God, give me my joy back. God, give me a new beginning!' And yes, prayer is important, but it's only part of the process. What really causes God to act is when you do something about it. You get back up, dust yourself off, and say, "You know what? I'm not going to stay down. This is the day the Lord has made. I am going to be happy and have a great day." That's putting action behind your faith.

I encourage you today to let your actions give life to your faith. Show the world that you are trusting God's Word. As you do, you'll give life to your faith and step into new levels of His victory and blessing in every area of your life

Father, thank You for Your Word that builds faith in my heart and refreshes my soul. I choose to put action behind my faith today. I choose to give life to my faith so that You can accomplish Your will in me. In Jesus' name, Amen.

Power Over the Clay

God has power over the clay
To mold you in his perfect way
He's the potter with a gentle hand
When he shape you, you will stand.

Stand tall and brave upon the land
With a firm foundation not one made of sand
When you sway against the breeze
He will right you again with ease.

The Potter has power of the clay
And he can reshape you in a marvelous way
Though you think you're hard to fit
He is patient at the wheel he'll sit.

God's the potter with power over the clay
He will mold you in a special way
You will be like no other here below
For he knows your purpose, and his plan he'll show.

God has power over the clay
He determines how long on the wheel we'll stay
Each clump of clay he will carefully measure
To place in our hearts the gifts we will treasure.

Yes, God has power over the clay.
When he lifts you off the wheel he'll pray
That you use the gifts he's placed in your heart
To give others a heavenly start.

Plant Your Seed

Plant a seed against your need
Have the faith the size of a mustard seed
Do it for a debt you owe
If you plant the seed it will grow.

Though you may not have a dime
Plant your seed as a source of time
God will give you what you need
There's no failure. He will succeed.

People are not your source to call
For they will falter, stumble or fall
Place your faith in the one who knows
He will reward you as your seed grows.

You must have patience – learn to watch and wait
Your blessing will come it will not be late
Take time out and praise your king
Lift up your voice and to him sing.

Plant your seed against your need
Watch my God. He will succeed
Your need will be filled without a doubt
It's your faith in him that this is about.

Good

Good: morally excellent or virtuous.

"Wish good for those who harm you; wish them well and do not curse them." – Romans 12:14.

It would be hard to find someone worse than Judas. Some say he was a good man with a backfired strategy. The Bible says Judas was a thief (John 12:6). The man was a crook. Somehow, he was able to live in the presence of God and experience the miracles of Christ and remain unchanged. In the end he decided he'd rather have money than a friend, so he sold Jesus for thirty pieces of silver. Judas was a scoundrel, a cheat, and a bum. How could anyone see him any other way?

We will condemn a person for doing bad things. We will soon forget whatever good they may have done in the past. It is all forgotten, and we will only remember the bad. We often times cannot forgive and then we have placed our lives in the hands of Satan. But Jesus was able to see something good in Judas. Only inches from the face of his betrayer, Jesus looked at him and said, *"Friend, do what you came to do."* – Matthew 26:50. What Jesus saw in Judas as worthy of being called a friend, I can't imagine. But I do know that Jesus doesn't lie, and in that moment he saw something good in a bad man.

He can help us do the same with those who hurt us. We love to sing this song:

"There's not a friend like the lowly Jesus:
No, not one! No, not one.
None else could heal all our soul's diseases
No, not one. No, not one!"

Jesus knows all about your struggles. He will surely guide you around every obstacle, circumstance, and condition in your life. He has not and will never forget you.

Doing Good

"Do not forget to do good and to share with others, for with such sacrifices God is pleased." – Hebrews 13:16 (NIV)

Many years ago, a former student stopped by my office with a Christmas gift. As she handed me the paper bag, she smiled and thanked me for the study tips I had given her during the semester. Because I knew that she and her family often struggled to pay her tuition and other college costs, I had not expected a gift from her. I opened the bag and pulled out the gifts: an apple, an orange, and a large peppermint candy stick. The student said that she wanted to buy something more expensive, but that these gifts were all she could afford. I received several other gifts that Christmas, but I have always remembered this former student's generosity.

Just as the young woman shared with me, God gives us opportunities to share and is pleased when we extend kindness to others. Today we can reach out to people In simple ways: a phone call, a hug, or a kind word. By doing good and sharing with others, we show our gratitude for God's love and mercy.

It does not matter what the gift you give, as long as you give the gift in love. Big price tags does not necessarily make better gifts.

Today, I will look for ways to share God's love.

Prayer: Dear Lord, teach me how to share your love with others. Amen.

Press Beyond the Crowd

Sometimes you have to press beyond the crowd
And do it without saying a single word out loud.
I've read of a woman who wanted to call out
Lift up her voice and let out a shout
She suffered and bled for twelve long years
I am sure she had to wipe away tears
She had gone to all the doctors she knew
And her funds had dwindled down to a few.

She had no doubt heard about Jesus being able to heal
She knew she had to touch him – so he would feel
The pain she bore and all her fears
All the anguish she shed through her tears
Her voice did not have to be lifted up and loud
But if she had to call his name she would not be too proud.

She was told my others her healing could be bought
She had no more money – so it was Jesus she sought
For she had faith and she did believe
That if she trusted in Jesus she would receive.

I will not allow anyone to get in my way
For I am counting on a miracle today
Lord, I'm moving toward you and the people are loud
I'm determined to press beyond this crowd.

Brenda C. Smith   49

I know it's your face I need not see
I know it's the hem of your garment that will heal me
For I need but place my hand on your hem
But I must press beyond all of them.

Wait on me Lord I will not falter
For my healing we don't need an altar
I am filled with faith from on high
And I heard you would be passing by
My faith in you will give me one last try
For when I touch the hem of your garment this disease will die.

The Cross

The Cross is usually thought of as a symbol of the Christian faith. Jesus was crucified on the cross on Calvary or Golgotha Hill. There is a vertical and a horizontal line. The vertical is upright, whereas, the horizontal is lying down or resting. Together this shows a symbol of manifestation. Manifestation is the act of demonstrating, a sign. Would you not agree? that the crucifixion was a demonstration of public feeling? The crowd had gathered around Jesus and cried, Crucify Him! Crucify Him! The cross stands for the uprightness of the truth and the down fall of falsehoods, lies and deceit. Truth is that which lives, which remains, which stands upright. False is that which falls, which is dead. If a person tells a lie on you, let it fall. Don't give the lie life by trying to defend it. Let it go.

Crosses symbolize spirituality and healing. The four points of a cross represent: self, nature, wisdom, and higher power. Crosses suggest transition, balance, faith, unity, temperance, hope and life. They represent relationships and a need to connect to something. The Cross symbolizes the religion of Christianity. It represents and memorializes Christ's death.

The empty cross reminds us Christians of the resurrection, while the crucifix, with the body of Jesus on it reminds us of Christ's sacrifice. I hope you all enjoy the beauty of this season. With all the colorful decorations, the eggs, the food, the gathering together in celebration. But, I want us all to remember that we are debt-free. Jesus through His sacrifice paid the cost and the debt has been cancelled. It is all to Him we owe. Let us walk in the "newness" of life. *"Therefore, if any man be in*

Christ, he is a new creature: old things are passed away; behold, all things are become new." – 2 Corinthians 5:17. Get rid of all those things that have you bound and enjoy this new lease on LIFE!! Happy Easter!!!

Victory in the Cross

Now that Easter Day is over and Good Friday has past, I want you to think about a very powerful thing that truly occurred "IN THE CROSS." We as Christians know, that Jesus died "ON THE CROSS," and we have to accept it by faith of and on the authority of Scripture. But, there was an invisible and remarkable phenomenon that happened IN THE CROSS that no one saw with their physical eye, but we can thank God for EASTER every day!

IN THAT CROSS the enemy of your soul was disrobed and disarmed. By means of that obscene instrument of execution the accuser of the brethren was put to open and public shame. It was at Calvary that our Lord triumphed over every demonic entity. This truth you know, *"He that is in you is greater than he who is in the world."* – I John 4:4. How this invisible victory was won through the visible agony of a man ON A CROSS that gives us victory IN THE CROSS.

Easter is simply His way of reminding us that we fight a defeated foe! Our enemy has received a deadly blow, his judgment has come, his doom is sealed. Though still prowling about as a roaring lion seeking whom he may devour his authority and power have been checked and his days are numbered. We are engaged in a war, the outcome of which, has already been decided in our favor! We fight an enemy over whom we have complete authority and from whom we need fear nothing. He has been convicted, sentenced to death, and is but for a season out on bail. Glory to God! That's what Easter did! Hallelujah!

How we glory in the cross. This lets me know that God is searching for what is on the inside of us that will make us and not break us. We were not there to witness the crucifixion of Jesus Christ. We did not see him hanging on the cross and all the agony he went through. Even back then we had our doubting Thomas. He said he would not believe it until he felt the nail prints in His hand. We have our scripture the breathed Word of God to assure us that it did in fact happen. Some folks say, "If I don't see it, I won't believe it?" Others tune in with, "I believe it, because I see it." Then there's the group that has the belief in their hearts that say, "Even though I did not see it, I believe it because God's Word said it." We don't have the tangibility of see, touch and feel. But we do have the truth in knowing that whatever God said in His Word is true. For he is not a man that he should lie, nor the son of man that he should repent (Numbers 23:19).

The Cross
(a poem)

When you look at your cross
Can you tell me what you see?
Do you see all the love
Christ had for you and me?

For on the cross he suffered
His body wracked with pain
But is there something else you see
A life you too can gain.

The price he pad for my sins
I will never comprehend
The magnitude of his giving
That he chose me over living.

For my cross is a symbol of Jesus
Giving up the ghost
The cross is empty. He's in heaven.
To welcome and to host.

God placed on his body
A robe in sparkling white
And I can hardly wait
To behold this glorious sight.

So, this cross that you see
It is beautiful to behold
For it is a symbol of his sacrificial love
And it means to the world I can't be bought or sold.

Giving Your Last –
Can Become Your Best

A widow woman in "I Kings" had but one meal of bread
When Elijah asked her to give it to him instead
She said it was her last, but it ended up her best
Because the Man of God put her faith to the test.

She went along her way and was unsure
For she and her son had much to endure.
She had no food and no more water to give
But for she and her son and no longer to live
Elijah said, "I need some water and a small piece of bread."
If you give it to me you will always be fed.

I need more than meal. I need water, too.
I need more than a promise of what you will do
Elijah said, "Promises I make with the Lord above
And whatever he says he will bless because of love."

If you feed me the meal and give your faith a try
God will bless you, when he hears your cry
She did not understand all that he said
But she gave him the water and the small cake of bread.

Elijah said the Lord will bless you with rain
No longer will you feel any hunger pain
For the Lord blesses you with the faith you need
And he will not let you want. You are his seed.

Elijah was the prophet sent to give her faith a test
He made her believe her last was her best
So be faithful and believe when you give to ones in need
That the one you are feeding is one who planted the seed.

The Holy Spirit

The Holy Spirit has always been a part of the Triune God. Now, as the Spirit lives in human beings, the Spirit is the life of God among us. The Spirit was there at the beginning (Genesis 1:2–3, 2:7). In the Old Testament the Spirit led people for special tasks: in particular, various prophets, priests and kings of Israel were gifted by the Spirit. He is the third divine person of the Trinity: the "Triune God" manifested as Father, Son, and Holy Spirit; each aspect itself being God.

Jesus was uniquely filled with the Holy Spirit (John 1:32–34; 7:37–39). He promised that the Spirit, his "other self," would come and live in believers after his death (John 14:15–18; 16:7–15). This came true at Pentecost (Acts 2). The Spirit lives in all believers; he does not withdraw from us, but remains with us; and he is no longer impersonal but marked with the imprint of Jesus.

The Holy Spirit is your friend.

When Jesus was here on the earth in the flesh, he was our helper, advocate, and meditator. But when he told his disciples he had to leave them, but he would "I will pray the Father…" (John 14:12). He was going to the Father to prepare a place for them. It was becoming clear that He was going away. How His heart must have ached for these dear friends, who were troubled and confused because they felt he was abandoning them.

The Holy Spirit is a person because he possesses a mind, emotions, and a will. The Holy Spirit thinks and knows (I Corinthians 2:10). The Holy Spirit can be grieved (Ephesians 4:30). The Spirit intercedes for us (Romans 8:26–27). He makes decisions according to His will.

We see the Holy Spirit's presence in many ways: through scripture, our spiritual gifts, the work of the church, and our life circumstances. These two symbols are associated with the Holy Spirit in Christian iconography: a winged dove and tongues of fire. The first symbol being represented of Jesus being baptized in the Jordan River where the Holy Spirit descended in the form of a dove as the voice of God the Father spoke. The second being represented as tongues of fire as described in Acts from the day of Pentecost, when the descent of the Holy Spirit came upon the Apostles and other followers of Jesus Christ.

Jesus' promise of the Spirit is all wrapped up in His declaration that He would "pray the Father." It is the opening of a new chapter in the dealings of God with mankind, in which the Holy Spirit is profoundly at work in people of all nations for the glory of the Son and to the worship of the Father.

Holy Spirit
(a poem)

I love you Holy Spirit
You're always by my side
To keep me from trouble
You are my daily guide.

Your presence engulfs me
And it always draw me near
When I am frightened
You whisper, "There's no need to fear."

You made it possible for me not to be alone
You gave me your saving power
That reaches out to me
Everyday and every hour.

I can talk to you any time I wish
And then I hear you talking back
There is nothing of you I cannot ask
For you will not cause me to lack.

Magnify me Jesus fill me with your spirit
I need your strength to face each day
For I know you will not fail me
But lead me home one day.

Brenda C. Smith   **59**

Is World Peace Really a Dream?

Is world peace really a dream?
And why are things not as they seem?
Do I have to dream of peace?
When will all the turmoil cease?

Are the olive branches on the trees all dead?
And we have been given sticks of wood instead.
It was good when Noah built the ark
We need world peace. This is no lark!

Each country looks at who has more might
Instead of how they appear in God's sight
Look at the person's character that's within
There's more to each person than the color of its skin.

Fighting each other for the rights to own their land
While others are starving and dying in the sand
Join hands around the world and pray for peace
Let go of hatred – allow its release.

Be a united nation to give hope that will last
Not a nation united to hold on to the past
Be a leader and a nation that chooses well
If not, you're leading all your people to hell.

Grab the olive branch given to the dove
Spread peace, happiness and above all love
Don't settle for peace found only in a dream
When you are awaken all will not be as it seemed.

Make peace a reality, instead of a dream
Peace should flow like water running in a stream
Make it fill your soul and cause an overflow
It will rise up to heaven and the whole world will know.

Put the Glass Down

A psychologist walking around the room was teaching stress management to an audience. As she raised a glass of water, everyone expected they'd be asked the "half empty or half full" question. Instead, with a smile on her face, she inquired: "How heavy is this glass of water?"

Answers called out range from 8 to 20 ounces.

She replied, "The absolute weight does not matter. It depends on how long I hold it. If I hold it for a minute, it's not a problem. If I hold it for an hour, I'll have an ache in my arm. If I hold it for a day, my arm will feel numb and paralyzed. In each case, the weight of the glass doesn't change, but the longer I hold it, the heavier it becomes!'

She continued, "The stresses and worries in life are like that glass of water. Think about them for a while and nothing happens. Think about them a bit longer and they begin to hurt. And if you think about them all day long, you will feel paralyzed – incapable of doing anything."

Remember to put the glass down.

The Greatest Love

The greatest love I've ever know
Is the greatest love my Jesus has shown
The day he died on Calvary's hill
My debt erased he paid the bill.

The cross was heavy – the hill was steep
The love in his heart for me ran deep
Nails were driven in both hands and feet
And for me he died when he took my seat.

He told his disciples this day had to be
It was the only way to save you and me
He had to suffer and pay the price
Jesus was the lamb and He the sacrifice.

I tremble when I think of all he had to suffer
He gave his life as the human buffer
He stood at the threshold between life and death
I was in his thoughts when he drew his last breath.

Yes, the greatest love I've ever known
Is the greatest love my Jesus has shown
The day he died on Calvary's hill
My debt erased he paid the bill.

The Struggle Is Real

The reality is that many normal Christians walk away from their faith for periods of time, for whatever reason. Challenges and temptation spin people around and bring them to their knees. Especially where hurt, shame, doubt, or lack of support is involved, It's easy to walk or run away from the faith-based life. But what about our testimonies? Have we forgotten we are to be witnesses in the earth?

It's Time to Get Real

The way we do testimonies needs to change. If we are still trying to make church, faith, and Christian living real, testimonies need to get real, too. We can't act like our struggles magically disappeared when we accepted Christ. Anything but the truth does a disservice to ourselves, to truth, and to each other. People can identify with struggle. We all are struggling on one level or the other. But it is the testimonies that we are able to share with others that God will use to strength them. Do not be ashamed, or afraid to let others know you have been through things. One of the biggest reasons people stay away from Church is because they think the ones there are "perfect!' They think they are not allowed to struggle.

Struggle is a reality. Temptation is a reality. Failure is a reality. Yes, even for those who are actively walking with Christ.

We can and should work to change Christian culture so that struggle doesn't have to be so embarrassing. The reality of Christ is shame isn't ours to bear (Isaiah 61:7). The reality of living in faith is Christians need to support each other. Ephesians 4:5–6 – *"One Lord, one faith, one baptism, One God and Father of all, who is above all, and through all, and in you all."* Telling real testimonies are key for that.

When Christians relay their stories, these stories become powerful turning points that happened along the road that built their faith and trust in God. Allow others to witness through your life and your testimony just how good God is. You do not have to share it with the world: within your ministry groups and within your family. Some family members think we who are strong never struggle, because we continue to take everything on. Share your testimony with a stranger. You can see their struggle with addictions: alcohol, drugs, or food. We have not always been saved. We have been in the world, so we need to witness to those who can benefit from the testimony of Jesus Christ.

Faint Not

"I will give you rain in due season, and the land shall yield her increase and the trees in the field yield their fruit." – Leviticus 26:4 (AMP)

God has set up seasons in our lives. There are plowing seasons. There are planting seasons. There are watering seasons. Sure, we would love for every season to be a time of increase left and right with good breaks everywhere. But without the other seasons, we wouldn't be prepared. For example, it's during the plowing season that God brings issues to light we need to deal with. He's getting us prepared for promotion.

If you're not making as much progress as you would like, the key is to not lose any ground. Don't go backwards. Hold your position. Keep a good attitude and do the right thing even when it's hard. When you do that, you are passing the test, and God promises that your due season of harvest is coming. Be encouraged because your appointed time of increase, favor and promotion is on its way. He's preparing you for the harvest to see every dream and every desire fulfilled in Jesus' name.

Hold on, you shall reap a harvest, if you do not faint!

Easter Story

Little Easter Story: A Sunday School teacher was having an Easter Egg Hunt for her class. She had both hard-boiled eggs and the plastic eggs with goodies inside. She decided to do an experiment with the students. She gave everyone an empty plastic egg and asked them to find something from outside to place inside the egg and bring it back to the class for discussion. They charged out the door into the yard and started to hunt for their eggs. She saw them stop and put things in their empty egg. When all of them got back in class she excitedly asked, "How did you do? Did everyone get something placed inside their empty egg?" They all said, "yes!" She noticed Philip did not respond but was somewhat excited to have his egg examined. She started with the front of the class and asked for one egg to be given to her to open.

She opened it, and there was a blade of grass – new growth. She opened another and a flower – Springtime. She opened another – a leaf, and she thought this is so good. Spring, new growth, and renewal. She noticed Philip was standing up, and she asked for his egg. He brought it to her and when she opened it, it was empty. The class erupted in laughter. They laughed and laughed. Someone said, "It is empty. Nothing is in there!" So, she asked Phillip, "Why did you give me an empty egg? Could you not find anything outside to fill it with?" He said, "When my father reads the story of the crucifixion in the Bible and tells me of the death of Jesus, he tells me that the best part of Easter is not the cross Jesus died on but the empty tomb that He was raised from. So when you asked us to place something inside the egg, I thought of the Bible story. When I opened the egg and saw it was empty, I remembered the tomb of Jesus." Like this empty egg, the tomb of Jesus is empty because HE IS RISEN!

Encourage

Encourage: To call to one's side; to help, console, strengthen, or comfort.

"Blessed be the God and Father of our lord Jesus Christ, the Father of mercies and God of all comfort, who comforts us in all our tribulations, that we may be able to comfort those who are in any trouble, with the comfort with which we ourselves are comforted by God." – 2 Corinthians 1:3–4.

Although it may seem like a trap from which there is no escape, every believer has a choice to either stay in a pit of discouragement or get out. It all depends on your perspective. If we focus on our difficult circumstances and negative feelings, we can easily be drawn into despair and depression. But, when we fix our eyes on our great, encouraging God, He lifts us up and sets us free. In Romans 15:4–5 Paul says that God gives both perseverance and encouragement so that we can have hope. Perseverance is the determination to keep going and not give up, whereas encouragement inspires, motivates and energizes. When we let the Lord encourage us, we'll have the energy, desire, and strength to endure whatever hardship we're facing.

A key element in overcoming discouragement is having a personal understanding of who God is and how He operates. Once we identify His attributes and recognize they were manifested to us through His indwelling spirit, we'll have a reason to be hopeful, even in trying situations. Our God is omnipotent, so we never have to wonder whether He is able to handle our situation. He is more than enough for whatever we're facing. Our God is omniscient and He possesses all knowledge. He has the answers to all our problems and is able to give perfect guidance for every situation. Our God has omnipresence. We are never out of God's reach, because He is everywhere. Even in times of loneliness and rejection, we are not alone since His Spirit lives within us.

There is no need to stay in a state of discouragement, because the Lord's attributes clearly reveal His desire to encourage us. No matter where we are or what we're doing, He's with us, working everything out for our benefit. Be encouraged.

Temporary

Temporary: not permanent. Having a limitation.

All the happiness and misery of the present state, resulting from things that are seen, are intermingled with contrary ingredients. We are never so happy in this world, as to have no uneasiness; in the greatest affluence we languish for some absent good, or grieve under some incumbent evil. On the other hand, we are never so miserable as to have no ingredient of happiness. When we labor under a thousand calamities, we may still see ourselves surrounded with, perhaps, an equal number of blessings. But in eternity every thing is everlasting and unchangeable.

Whatever you are dealing with today that is getting you down, know today it is temporary. It has an expiration date as to how long it shall haunt you, invade your life, disturb your peace, and keep you awake at night. God has already stamped an end to it, long before you were even born. Take heart today and live in hope. But when we pass out of this transitory state, we enter upon an everlasting state. Our souls will always exist; exist in a state of unchangeable, boundless happiness or misery. It is but a little while since we came into being out of a state of eternal non-existence, but we shall never relapse into that state again.

Hold on and believe that God has you in the very palm of His hand. Whatever, it is He is working it out for your good (Romans 8:28). And we know that all things work together for our good! Psalm 84:11 – *"Lord God is a sun and shield and He will give grace and glory, no good thing will He withhold from them who walk uprightly."* That is a promise that God will forever keep with His children.

Miracles

"Believe in me for the sake of the work themselves," – John 14:11.

Sooner or later, everyone will face a crisis that they cannot manage. There will come a point in your life when the only hope you have left in this world will be a miracle. But, I have good news, our God is still a miracle-working God. Our God breathed life into the dead womb of Sarah and nine months later, she and Abraham became parents to Isaac. That is a miracle. The same God that parted the Red Sea for Moses and rained manna from the heavens for the children of Israel for forty years is the same miracle-working God today!

Maybe your crisis will come in the form of an attack on your health, but our God is the Healer! Jesus healed the lame, deaf and the blind. He restored the paralytic and raised dead men from the grave. Consider this: the Word of God says that "Jesus Christ is the same yesterday, today and forever." You must know that what He did on the shores of the Sea of Galilee, He can do for you today.

Some Christians don't ask for their miracles because they do not understand miracles. First, it is important that you realize you do not have to understand miracles in order to receive a miracle. Do you completely understand how food is converted into energy when you eat it? Does that mean that you are going to stop eating food until you do? Are you going to live in darkness just because you cannot fully understand how electricity works? Surely not, if you are willing to experience only what your carnal mind can understand, then you will live a shallow and empty life, and you will never experience a miracle.

Revival Is You

Revival is for you. *"Will you not revive us again, that your peopla may rejoice in you."* – Psalm 85:6.

The three P's of Revival: PRAYER, PRAISE, and PROCLAIM. We are the house and the temple of the Lord. We have to first humble ourselves and pray. 2 Chronicles 7:14 – *"If my people which are called by my name shall humble themselves and pray, seek my face, turn from their wicked ways, then will I hear."* Two catch phrases there: "If" and "turn." We want God to hear our prayers when we pray, answer them when we pray, but we do not want to humble ourselves and turn from our wickedness in order for Him to do so.

Praise for God inhabits the praise of His people. When God has done something for you, you ought to praise His name. God did not have to do it, but thank Him because He did. When we praise God, our Jericho walls fall and the walls are flatten so we can walk across to blessed land. And proclaim simply means we ought to tell somebody of the deliverance that God has given us. We tell everything but the good news of Jesus Christ. We are His ambassadors down here. We holler louder at a sporting event for players who have done nothing for us and we can't hear a praise from you in church to a God who has done everything.

BUY THE TRUTH AND SELL THE LIE.

We will not buy into the truth of Jesus Christ being the Savior of the world, but we will sell the lie everywhere we go that the devil is not defeated. That is an easy sell, because the devil wants to hear that lie. Glory to God!

Rescue

Rescue: keep from being lost or stolen. Retrieved. (Ephesians 1:3–12)

Two Horses

Just up the road from my home is a field with two horses in it. From a distance, each looks like every other horse. But if you stop your car or are walking by, you will notice something quite amazing. Looking into the eyes of one horse will disclose that he is blind.

His owner has chosen not to have him put down, but he has made a good home for him. This alone is amazing. If nearby and listening, you will hear the sound of a bell. Looking around for the source of the sound, you will see it comes from the smaller horse in the field. Attached to her halter is a small bell, it lets her blind friend know where she is, so he can follow her.

As you stand and watch these two friends, you'll see how she is always checking on him, and that he will listen for her bell and then slowly walk to where she is, trusting that she will not lead him astray. When she returns to the shelter of the barn each evening, she stops occasionally and looks back, making sure her friend isn't too far behind to hear the bell.

Author Unknown

Like the owner of these two horses, God does not throw us away just because we are not perfect or because we have problems or challenges. He watches over us and even brings others into our lives to help us when we are in need. Sometimes, we are the blind horse being guided by the little ringing bell of those who God places in our lives. Other times we are the guide horse, helping others see. Good friends are like this. You don't always see them, but you know they are always there.

Please listen for my bell, and I'll listen for yours.

Your "Go To" Person

This is Jesus speaking, *"Beloved, I know sometimes it is hard facing the things before you. Consider this: I lived where you now live. The emotional abuse and the lack of understanding sometimes became overwhelming. I had a person to go to. When it became unbearable, I went to our Father."* Remember this when your life becomes unbearable. You too have the same "go to" person, but now I am with you to explain to Him in detail how it is. I'm your advocate. I say things that explain people and events in both worlds: on earth and in heaven.

"Therefore, since we have a great high priest who has gone through the heavens, Jesus the Son of God, let us hold firmly to the faith we profess. For we do not have a high priest who is unable to sympathize with our weaknesses, but we have one who has been tempted in every way, just as we are, yet was without sin. Let us then approach the throne of grace with confidence, so that we may receive mercy and find grace to help us in our time of need." – Hebrews 4:14–16 (NIV).

Breath

Breath: air inhaled and exhaled in respiration. Especially needed for life.

"God's breath of life gives man his lifeblood, and 'the breath of the Almighty gives him understanding.'" – Job 32:8.

Your breath is not your own. The Spirit of God made me, and the breath of the Almighty gives me life (Job 33:4). If you are reading this devotional, you are breathing. Let us thank Him. We breathe in and out, and it seems to be a simple thing to do, but it is controlled by our nervous system. Breathing is regulated by the respiratory center of the brain and more than twenty respiratory muscles. In all the things that man can boast about creating, he did not create breath. It is a gift of God. He is the originator of the process and begins and sustains life.

"And the lord God formed man of the dust of the ground, and breathed into his nostrils the breath of life; and man became a living being." – Genesis 2:7. Why don't you thank Him today for His breath being in your body.

Make this the day you inspect your own breath of life. If there's any false pride that's arisen, remember that man doesn't own anything, including his own breath. What we have is from God's gracious hand, and only what we give back to Him will live and breathe forever.

Hard

Hard: difficult to deal with or understand.

"On hearing it, many of his disciples said, 'This is a hard teaching. Who can accept it?' Aware that his disciples were grumbling about this, Jesus said to them, 'Does this offend you?'" – John 6:60–61.

It does not matter how hard and laborious the delivery was when a woman delivers her child; all pain ceases when she sees that precious face and holds that tiny hand. The joy of that moment is so intense and sweet that the pain does not dull it a minute. We must then follow Jesus even though His words are hard. Grumbling is not a new response to God and his ways. After he brought them out of Egypt, the Israelites complained about the difficulties of their lives and their misfortunes. And God was displeased. Jesus recognizes the issue is the hardness of their heart, not the harshness of His words.

First, we must admit the words are hard, and yet stay with Jesus. The difficulties are no different or less today than they were when Jesus spoke. In John 6, Jesus makes clear that He is God's son, fully God and yet fully man. They understood they just did not like it. They did not like the exclusivity of Jesus' divinity: *"If you have seen me, you have seen the Father."* Jesus demands they come to God through him: *"No one comes to the Father except by me:'*

Second, we must call people with truth. Jesus does not compromise simply because people are offended. We also must not sell out in the hopes of selling Jesus. We do the work of evangelism, keeping before us – John 8.31: *"If you abide in my word, you are truly my disclples, and you will know the truth and the truth will set you free."* Truth is the Holy Spirit's means for breaking through hard hearts.

What they wanted, he would not give; what he offered, they would not receive.

Potholes

Potholes: hole in a rock, or pavement worn away by water.

"Receive one who is weak in the faith, but not to dispute over doubtful things." – Romans 14:1.

This is one thing I know all drivers have experienced. Driving over a pothole with ease, but there are times when you don't see it and a tire goes flat, and realignment is in order. Some of us try to avoid them by swerving. Still others try to roll over it easily. For those of us who do not see it comlng, well, let's just say, "Thank you, Jesus." Because it could have been worse. This is true of this Christian walk that we must do. We can become comfortable and settled-in and relaxed and start to feel we are moving along this road with ease; when all of a sudden, there is a bump in the road.

Three quick steps to follow on the road:

1. Drive Slowly – We must learn to be patient. When we hear the word "patient," "wait" comes to mind. *"But they that wait upon the Lord shall renew their strength; they shall mount up with wings as eagles; they shall run and not be weary; and they shall walk, and not faint."* – Isaiah 40:31.

2. Be Alert – We have to train ourselves to look out for danger. Satan is not going to let us live a comfortable life as Christians. He is always out to get us and bring us down.

3. Refuel – When you are walking this Christian walk, you must make sure you have plenty of fuel for the journey. No different than your car that needs gas to get from destination A to destination B. We need to make sure we are filled with the Word of God. We need to spend good quality time with the Lord! We need to understand that we cannot always just go in and say a quick prayer and all will be alright. Sometimes, we must fast and pray, and then meditate, too. Sometimes Saints, it truly takes all that and more to get the desired result. I believe we short circuit many of our blessings, by not being committed to what the Lord needs from us during a slowdown or rest.

Happy T.G.I.F. (Thank God It's Friday!)

Many of you have enjoyed a wonderful meal and sweet fellowship with your family and friends on Thanksgiving. Now, you are prepared to go out and do the Black Friday shopping and get gifts for the gift exchange on Christmas. Society is making your Thanksgiving shorter and shorter. Take a few minutes to see how society paints the picture. Black Friday is a day of rushing, pushing, and pulling, and people even loose control and cry out in anger if they do not get what they want from the suppliers. On Good Friday, the people complained, pushed, pulled, and cried out Crucify Him! Crucify Him! until they got Jesus placed upon the cross on Calvary's Hill.

Good Friday was a Black Friday, too, because the sun refused to shine. God could not look at the ugly sin that had been placed upon His Son for us. Jesus had no sin. But, He gave his all for us on Calvary. Don't get so caught up in the hype that you loose control out there and no one will be able to separate you from the unbelievers. You have integrity and dignity, and you are a Child of the Most High God. The great gift exchange has already been done for us. It happened over 2000 years ago. Isaiah 9:6 – *"For unto us a child is born, unto us a Son is given: and the government shall be upon his shoulder: and his name shall be called Wonderful, Counseller, The mighty God, The everlasting Father, The Prince of Peace."* He was born for you and me. And on Calvary's Hill the exchange was made. *"... and led him away to crucify Him."* – Matthew 27:31

Matthew 27:45–46 – *"Now from the sixth hour there was darkness over all the land unto the ninth hour. In the ninth hour, Jesus cried out. 'My God, my God, why hast thou forsaken me?'"* His Black Friday was to save humanity. The darkness of sin blinds people's heart to God. God has done everything to save our soul. Jesus Christ died to pay your death penalty. The rest of the story is He AROSE! HE LIVES TODAY! No gift purchased from a supplier in this world can ever take the place of what God has already given and for what Jesus has already done. His Black Friday.

Battle

Battle: a great struggle.

"For though we walk in the flesh, we do not war after the flesh: (For the weapons of our warfare are not carnal, but mighty through God to the pulling down of strong holds;) – 2 Corinthians 10:3–4.

Three simple truths: 1. I am a Child of God. 2. I am alive in Christ. 3. I am a new creation.

All of us agree these statements are true. If we are honest, we have all found ourselves wondering at one time or another, "If what the Bible tells me about my identity in Christ is true, then why do I still battle the same thoughts and feelings I had before I became a Christian? Why can't I break free from these things that haunt my mind?"

Would you like to know the answer to such questions as these? We have to win the battle of our minds. Although we live in the world, we do not wage war as the world does. The weapons we fight with are not the weapons of the world. On the contrary, they have divine power to demolish strongholds. We demolish arguments and every pretension that sets itself up against the knowledge of God. We take captive every thought to make it obedient to Christ.

So why do we still battle with the same thoughts and feelings that we had before we became a Christian? Paul said, "We are human, but we don't wage war with human plans and methods." We are now Christians, yet we still live in the world, but we don't go to war as the world does. This is our problem: the battle for our mind cannot be won using the same thinking we had before we accepted Christ. Yet, many of us still try to win the battle for our mind the same way we always did. As we grew from childhood to adults, we learned to respond to life in a variety of ways, but each response had one thing in common. We learned to go through life without God. We were unaware of His presence in our lives, and we did not know His ways. We learned to live our lives independent from God.

Release

Release: to be free from confinement, bondage, obligation, pain, etc; let go: to release a prisoner; to release someone from a debt. To free from anything that restrains, or fastens.

Saints, this is definitely your season of divine release. The Lord is granting total freedom from every entanglement created or planned for you by the devil. Mark 11:2–3 – *"And saith unto them, 'Go your way into the village over against you: and as soon as ye be entered into it, ye shall find a colt tied, whereon never man sat; loose him. and bring him. And if any man say unto you, Why do ye this? Say ye that the Lord hath need of him; and straightway he will send him hither.'"* Whenever there's divine release, some things have been found to be present that probably initiate the release. There went up a cry for help in your situation.

You must be tired of your present situation. You must rise above the frustration these problems have caused you. You being fed-up with your lack of freedom, and you need to be energized to become creative to get things done in a better way. It is when we are pushed to the wall that some of us come up with great ideas that shape the world. Your cry of help will initiate an intervention on God's part. Whenever you are in the bondage of the oppressor, cry out to the Lord, and He in turn will send a deliverer to release you from the hand of the oppressor. He did this many times in the Bible.

God remembers and He sets in motion a release to an individual or a group or even a nation. He remembered the covenant He had with Abraham. He sent a rescue mission led by Moses to release His people from Pharaoh. He remembered Noah and his family. He remembered Daniel in the lion's den. He remembered us and sent His Son to save and to die for us. God needs you for a certain purpose that only you can fulfill. He is in need of us to show compassion to our neighbors and to care for the sick, helpless, and weak among us. Start believing the Word of God is true, and that you will accomplish the works of Jesus and even greater works according to John 14:12-14. Let's get passionate about pursuing the things God has for us. Your Divine Release has been set in motion, and it is on its way in Jesus' name.

Foundations of Christianity

What is Christianity? It is not a religion, but a revelation and a rescue. It sets out to reveal to us what God is like – Creator (Genesis 1:1), Holy (Isaiah 6:3), and Love (I John 4:8). It shows us the lengths God is willing to go in order to rescue us (John 3:16, Mark 10:22–34). Christianity is not a matter of church-going, ceremonies, creeds or conduct, though it embraces all four. Christianity is Christ.

Jesus Christ is human, like us. He was born, lived, suffered and died – very human. But he was more-than-human. He was, as his name means, "God to the rescue" (Matthew 1:21). He was the fulfillment of all God had been showing his people in Israel for centuries. He is God's "Word," his message to us in the terms of a human life. He is light and in him is no darkness at all (I John 1:5).

The Great Commission:
Is It Still Needed?

The Great Commission:

Matthew 28:18–20 – *"Go ye therefore, and teach all nations, baptizing them in the name of the Father, and of the Son, and of the Holy Ghost: Teaching them to observe all things whatsoever I have commanded you: and, lo, I am with you alway, [even] unto the end of the world. Amen."*

First, these words are important because, at least in Matthew's gospel, they are the last words of Jesus. These words are important because they apply without exception to all Christians at all times, in all places, in every possible situation. The words of Jesus Christ have a permanent and enduring and universal validity for you and for me. That's why they were given, and that's why they were recorded. We ought to pay special attention to what Jesus is saying here.

If this is the Great Commission of Jesus Christ, then it should be our Great Commission, too. We are called to be Great Commission Christians and to build a Great Commission Church. We need to be like disciples, bringing people in.

The good mark of a healthy church is not the size of the budget, the size of the staff, the beauty of the choir, the glory of the music, the wonder of the architecture, or any of the worldly measures we like to use. The real and true mark of the church in Jesus' eyes is a church that is 100 percent dedicated to fulfilling the Great Commission. We are in the disciple-making process. Is your church doing this? Are your members equipping people to do this?

Nothing is more important than for us to be Jesus' kind of church and to be His kind of people who are working on kingdom building. The Great Commission is powered by the Holy Spirit. We are to be Christ's witnesses, fulfilling the Great Commission in our cities (Jerusalem), in our states and countries (Judea and Samaria), and anywhere else God sends us (to the ends of the earth).

Yes, the Great Commission is still needed. It is still alive. It is still necessary. It is still God speaking.

The Romans Road to Salvation

The Romans Road to salvation is a way of explaining the good news of salvation using verses from the Book of Romans.

Those Scriptures are Romans 3:23, *"For all have sinned, and come short of the glory of God."* Romans 3:10–18 gives a detailed picture of what sin looks like in our lives. The second Scripture on the Romans Road to salvation, Romans 6:23, teaches us about the consequences of sin – *"For the wages of sin is death; but the gift of God is eternal life through Jesus Christ our Lord."*

The third verse on the Romans Road to salvation picks up where Romans 6:23 left off, *"but the gift of God is eternal life through Jesus Christ our Lord."* Romans 5:8 declares, *"But God demonstrates His own love toward us, in that while we were still sinners, Christ died for us."* Jesus Christ died for us! Jesus' death paid for the price of our sins. Jesus' resurrection proves that God accepted Jesus' death as the payment of our sins.

The fourth stop on the Romans Road to salvation is Romans 10:9, *"that if you confess with your mouth Jesus as Lord, and believe in your heart that God raised Him from the dead, you will be saved."*

The final aspect of Romans Road to salvation is the results of salvation. Romans 5:1 has this wonderful message, *"Therefore, since we have been justified through faith, we have peace with God through our Lord Jesus Christ."* Through Jesus Christ we can have a relationship of peace with God. Romans 8:1 teaches us, *"Therefore, there is now no condemnation for those who are in Christ Jesus."* Amen.

What Does the Invitation of Christ Mean?

The first invitation is an invitation to rest.

Again and again in the Bible, people are graciously invited to enter into personal fellowship with God. Jesus said, *"Come unto Me, all you who labor and are heavy laden, and I will give you rest."* – Matthew 11:28. Since our bliss ended in the Garden of Eden, we have been a people of restlessness. When we are deprived of the peace that comes from God through the saving grace of Christ, we become like fish out of water.

The second invitation is to discipleship.

"Jesus said to them, 'Follow Me, and I will make you fishers of men'" – Mark 1:17. We are saved to serve; we are redeemed to reproduce spiritually; we are fished out of the miry clay so that we in turn become fishers of men. Christian discipleship gives us the privilege associated with Christ intimately. And the faithful discharging of the glorious responsibilities of true discipleship invokes the approval and favor of God Himself. *"If anyone desires to come after me,' said Jesus, 'let him deny himself, and take up his cross daily, and follow Me.'"* – Luke 9:23. A discipleship means a learner, a student, a follower. You learn discipleship from Christ. A true discipleship of Jesus Christ will bear the fruit of the Spirit: love, joy, peace, longsuffering, gentleness, goodness, faith, meekness, and temperance. (Galatians 5:22–23). People who are in contact with us on a daily basis will know we have been with Jesus. We will radiate Christ. The secret of the Christian life is Christ lives within us, producing fruit.

The third invitation is to live in the realm of God.

Jesus said, *"Abide in Me, and I in you."* – John 15:4. Personal salvation is not an occasional rendezvous with Deity; it is an actual dwelling with God. Christianity is not just an avocation; it is a lifelong, eternity-long vocation. David was so thrilled with the knowledge that his life was in God, he said in Psalm 91:1 – *"He who dwells in the secret place of the Most High shall abide under the shadow of the Almighty."* One of mankind's basic needs is security. You can be assured that in this Psalm God is our greatest security. *"No evil shall befall you, nor shall any plague come near your dwelling; for He shall give His angels charge over you, to keep you in all your ways."* – Psalm 91:10–11.

Another basic need is affection. Those who "abide in Him" are the objects of God's affection and love. The final basis need is the need to belong. God is inviting sinful men and women to be identified with Him in His great redemptive and creative work. No club of any kind in this world can compare with the knowledge of the fact that you belong to God and are identified with Him.

These three invitations are not mine. They are given by Jesus Himself. No man or woman has ever found complete rest apart from Christ. To the multitudes, to the masses, to the distressed, troubled, and weary He beckons, *"Come unto me, and I will give you rest."*

What Is Faith?

Faith is defined in the first verse of chapter of the Bible, Hebrews 11, *"Now faith is the substance of things hoped for, the evidence of things not seen."* It means persuasion, conviction of religious truth, conviction of the truthfulness of God, or reliance on God. This verse tells us that faith is assurance that we will receive the things for which we hope, and it supports the knowledge that we will receive them. The Bible has promises for blessings in this life if we obey God, and it also contains promises for eternal life in the kingdom of God. Faith is the assurance that we will receive those promises.

Faith is also the evidence of proof of what we cannot see or what we have not seen yet. By faith we know that God made the universe, although we cannot see God and were not present at the creation. Faith is the evidence or proof that God exists, and it is also the evidence that He will keep His promises, even though we have not seen those promises yet.

This verse does not define faith in terms of the five senses: sight, hearing, touch, smell, and taste. If we could perceive the object of our faith, we would not need faith.

Romans 4:16–21 describes the relationship that the Old Testament patriarch Abraham had with God: *"being fully convinced that what He had promised He was also able to perform."* Abraham had faith that God could keep His promises, and he was assured that he would receive them. He had the evidence, which is faith.

Let us consider what faith is not. Faith is not merely believing in Christ, John 8:31, *"Then said Jesus to those Jews which believed on him, If ye continue in my word, then are ye my disciples indeed."* They believed in Christ but did not believe His message.

How Do We Receive Faith? *"For by grace you have been saved through faith, and that not of yourselves; it is the gift of God." – Ephesians 2:5.* We are to live by Christ's faith in us – his gift to us.

Faith is a part of the fruit of God's Holy Spirit. Galatians 5:22–23 – *"But the fruit of the Spirit is love, joy, peace, longsuffering, gentleness, goodness, faith, meekness, temperance: against such there is no law."*

God may not answer our prayers immediately, if He did we would not need faith for very long. He may not come when we want Him, but He is always on time. If we have faith, we know that God is able to work miracles in our lives, that He can protect us physically and heal us. He will provide for our needs, and often He will even provide for our wants. Most importantly, by faith He will develop His holy, righteous character in us in order that we can become members of His family.

Hebrews 10:34–38 states, *"The just shall live by faith."* The Bible is full of promises for this life and for eternal life in the kingdom of God. God is looking for people who believe. Are you a believer in Jesus Christ?

Suddenly

Suddenly: happening unexpectedly; changing all at once; brought about in a short time.

"And suddenly a great tempest arose on the sea, so that the boat was covered with the waves. But, He was asleep." – Matthew 8:24.

We are in a season of the unexpected where the events that are happening around us may seem abrupt and illogical. However, I believe God is accelerating His end time purposes to bring about a restoration of His glory on the earth before the return of His Son Jesus. We as Christians are experiencing things on a much deeper level than ever before. Our main priority is to learn to trust in the Word of God like we have never had to in the past. We are to be tuned in, be vigilant, be prepared, be ready, and be expectant. We have to respond to the storms in our lives when we least expect them. We sometimes think Jesus is asleep , but remember, He is a Lord who never sleeps nor slumbers. He is ever vigilant, prepared, and ready to act in our lives in the blink of an eye.

We will from time to time get demands on our anointings and miracles will happen when we least expect them. Hallelujah! And suddenly, a woman who had a flow of blood for twelve years came from behind and touched the hem of His garment. God is trying to bring us from behind. We have gifts and anointings we are not using to our potential. He knows what each of us is capable of doing, and He needs us to start using them. Let us stop shrinking back and hiding behind excuses, people, and work. God's kingdom will be done on earth as it is in heaven. The Lord is doing a new thing on the earth, and it takes a prophetic generation to ride the wave of the Spirit. Let's be part of the movement!

Welcome trials, they're stepping stones to perfection (James 1:3).

No Test. No Testimony
Earn Stars through scars.
Make sure Jesus is in your boat.
He's never early, but neither will He be late.

Ask for Your Hedge of Protection

Satan stated to the Lord, "Have you not put a hedge of protection around him and his household and everything he has?" It is common for Christians to pray a "hedge of protection" around a family member, or friends. This is what it means.

In the Old Testament times wild animals were prevalent in the Middle East much more than they are today. The Bible mentions lions, wolves, bears, leopards, and hyenas. Although stone walls could keep predators away from living areas and livestock, the walls would have to be very tall and would take a long time to make. Wood was not plentiful enough to waste on a fence. Instead, a hedge of thorn bushes could be induced to grow around a living compound, home, or dwelling.

A hedge of thorn bushes would be too dense to crawl through, too sharp to chew through, and too deep for all but the most determined leopard to jump over. A hedge would also be a deterrent to sheep and goats seeking to escape their pen. As Satan is compared to a "lion looking for someone to devour" (I Peter 5:8), a thorn hedge is an appropriate metaphor for the protection God gives His followers.

Have you asked for your hedge of protection today? Ask for that same hedge that protected Job to protect you, your family, and friends. *"Therefore put on the full armor of God, so that when the day of evil comes, you may be able to stand your ground, and after you have done everything, to stand. Stand firm then, with the belt of truth buckled*

around your waist, with the breastplate of righteousness in place, and with your feet fitted with the readiness that comes from the gospel of peace. In addition to all this, take up the shield of faith, with which you can extinguish all the flaming arrows of the evil one. Take the helmet of salvation and the sword of the Spirit, which is the word of God." –
Ephesians 6:13-17 (NIV)

We can and should ask for the hedge of protection, too. There is nothing wrong with asking for protection from our enemies. It worked for Job, and that same hedge will work for you, too.

Excuse

Excuse: to seek or obtain exemption or release for oneself.

"And the people said to Joshua, 'The lord our God we will serve, and His voice we will obey!'" – Joshua 24:24

God doesn't want us to merely sit around dreaming about things we can do and be. That's a good place to start, but a poor place to stop. God wants us to turn our dreams into action. We all have untapped gifts and talents inside us, and the way to develop our potential is by stepping out in faith and making the most of every opportunity. It's not how much you have, but it's how you use what you have that matters. Are you making the most of the gifts and talents God has given to you?

God is not moved by excuses.

He's not inclined to help us when we feel sorry for ourselves. No, God is moved by faith. When we step out in faith and use the talents He's given us, we show that we trust God, that we believe He will bless our actions and cause us to succeed.

Sometimes, God presents opportunities that look insignificant, or rather ordinary. Perhaps you don't see how they fit into the big picture for your life. But if God is asking you to do something, He has a purpose for it. You just need to be faithful, and when you're diligent in handling the little things, God can increase and promote you to larger responsibilitiesby being faithful with what you've been given. You may think you're working at some meaningless job, or you're just raising your kids, or you're doing something that seems ordinary, it's not exciting; you can't see where it's leading you. Let me encourage you to be faithful. Stick with it. Give it your all. Keep a good attitude, and God will increase you. If you will be the best that you can be right where you are, God will promote you and give you more.

Understand that those silent times—those times when God is doing something in your life that doesn't seem to make sense—those are times of growth. God is working on your character. That's when God is preparing you, and if you'll be faithful and pass the test, you'll be ready for promotion.

The Eagle Story
(Isaiah 40:31)

Someone once told me a story about a wounded eagle who was rescued by a kindly farmer. He found the bird in one of his fields, and so he took him home, tended to his wounds, and then placed him outside in the barnyard to recover. Strangely enough, the young eaglet soon adapted to the habits of all the barnyard chickens. He learned to walk and cluck like them. He learned to drink from a trough and peck the dirt for food, and for many years he peacefully resigned himself to this new life on the ground.

But then one day, one of the farmer's friends spotted the eagle and asked, "Why in the world is that bird acting like a chicken?" The farmer told him what had happened, yet the man could hardly accept the situation. "It's just not right," said the friend, "The Creator made that bird to soar in the heavens, not scavenge in the barnyard." So he picked up the unsuspecting eagle, climbed onto a nearby fencepost, and tossed him into the air. But the confused bird just fell back to earth and scurried off in search of his feathered friends. Undaunted, the man then grabbed the eagle and climbed to the top of the barn. As he heaved him off the roof, the bird made a few halfhearted squawks and flaps before falling into a bale of hay. After shaking his head a few times, the eagle then made himself comfortable and began mindlessly pecking at pieces of straw.

The friend went home that night dejected and could barely sleep as he remembered the sight of those powerful talons caked with barnyard mud. He couldn't bear the thought, so the very next day, he headed back to the farm for another try. This time he carried the eagle to the top of a nearby mountain where the sky unfolded in a limitless horizon.

He looked into the eagle's eyes and cried out, "Don't you understand? You weren't made to live like a chicken. Why would you want to stay down here when you were born for the sky?" As the man held the confused bird aloft, he made sure the eagle was facing into the brilliant light of the setting sun. Then, he powerfully heaved the bird into the sky, and this time the eagle opened his wings, looked at the sun, caught the updraft rising from the valley, and disappeared into the clouds of heaven.

The Lord has called us to live in the heights, yet too many of us have huddled together in the barnyard, contentedly scurrying for the safety of our families, our finances, our careers and our comfortable crumbs of faith. God is asking us to spread our majesty wings and SOAR!

Hide

Hide: yo conceal from sight; prevent from being seen.

"He shall cover you with His feathers, And under His wings you shall take refuge; His truth shall be your shield and buckler." – Psalm 91:4 (NKJV)

After a forest fire in Yellowstone National Park, forest rangers began their trek up a mountain to assess the inferno's damage. One ranger found a bird literally petrified in ashes, perched as a stature on the ground at the base of a tree. Somewhat sickened by the eerie sight, he knocked over the mother's wings. The loving mother, keenly aware of impending disaster, had carried her offspring to the base of a tree and had gathered them under her wings, instinctively knowing that the toxic smoke would rise. She could have flown away to safety but had refused to abandon her babies. When the blaze had arrived and the heat had singed her small body, the mother had remained steadfast. Because she was willing to die, those under the cover of her wings would live.

Does this story remind you of the everlasting love of our Lord and Savior? How he went to the cross and died for your sins and mine. How he could have come down from the cross and rescued himself, but like the mother bird he chose to take the anguish and pain; even to die to cover and protect us. Jesus Christ has us at the foot of the cross where we are shielded by His Word and are covered by His blood.

Charge

Charge: to make a debt. To defer a payment for a debt until payment is received.

"Thus the heavens and the earth, and all the host of them, were finished." – Genesis 2:1.

A little girl was sitting on Santa's lap. She gave him a whole list of expensive toys which she wanted for Christmas and then without a word of appreciation, she jumped off Santa's lap and started toward her mother. Her concerned mother spoke quickly, "Honey, haven't you forgotten something?" The little girl thought for a moment, then said, "Oh, yes," Then turning back toward Santa, she shouted, "Charge it!"

A work was finished in Christ. God completed His work of creation by declaring it is finished. Jesus Christ did the same thing. When He completed His work on earth, His atoning work on the cross, He cried, "It is finished." When Jesus said, "It is finished," He declared that everything necessary for salvation was complete. We can add nothing to His finished work. He is the author and finisher of salvation. It is His work, His grace, and His love that saves us. And it was His sacrifice that made it possible. It made it possible for us to not only be saved, but to stay saved. For just like the fact that we can add nothing to His finished work, we can take nothing away from His finished work. Just like it is His work that saves us, it is His work that keeps us saved. His grace keeps us saved. And His love keeps us saved. Philippians 1:6 says, *"Being confident of this very thing, that He which hath begun a good work in you will perform it until the day of Jesus Christ."* Jesus began a good work in you. He is performing a good work in you. All because He has already finished His work on the cross. He's finished all the work that is necessary. The work is finished. It's finished in creation, and it's finished in Christ. But not only was a work finished, a rest was entered. The second parallel between the finished work of God in creation, and the finished work of Christ on the cross is that a rest was entered. Jesus did the hard part so we could rest from our cares, worries, labor, stress, and strife. Let's not be like the little girl. The work is finished. Let's say, "Thank You!"

Guilt

Guilt: having done wrong.

"For whosoever shall keep the whole law, and yet offend in one point, he is guilty of all." – James 2:10. *"But God commandeth his love toward us, in that, while we were yet sinners, Christ died for us."* – Romans 5:8–9.

The first thing we need to understand is there are things for which we should feel guilty, and there are things for which we should not feel guilty. There are things for which we should feel guilty and take personal responsibility. However, there is false guilt where we carry the guilt of what other people have done. False guilt cripples us, and the truth is we do not wish to carry what is not ours. Recognize this fact and assign it, appropriately. Guilt can have either a positive or negative effect in and on our lives. Positively, it can bring us to take responsibility, seek forgiveness and experience freedom.

Guilt can lie dormant for years in our hearts and then all of a sudden come to the surface, sometimes with such force that it feels like we are drowning. Guilt can be triggered years later by a memory, a meeting, and we need to have in place the Biblical understanding of how to deal with it when it does appear. When these times come, we must remember that Jesus Christ has paid the debt for all our sin. This means that He has already paid the price for our wrongdoing, and we have been found "not guilty." As our sin lies dead at the cross, so does our guilt.

What did this loving act accomplish? It enabled us to approach almighty God as clean, pure, and holy men and women. Our purity is not related to anything we ourselves have done; it is due exclusively to the fact that we have been purified in Jesus' blood. That's why we can say we have been "washed in the blood," which is the only way the stain of sin can be removed.

Thank you Heavenly Father today, not only for forgiving our sin, but also for freeing us from the burden of guilt. Thank you for providing the only way out. You gave the perfect sacrifice: Your Son, Jesus Christ (Romans 5:8).

Let's rejoice in knowing this emotional pain is no longer ours to carry.

Blessed

Blessed: to be blessed is to be "made holy" or consecrated (dedicated to a divine purpose).

"Blessed be the God and Father of our Lord Jesus Christ, who has blessed us with every spiritual blessing in the heavenly places in Christ." – Ephesians 1:3.

Whenever we hear the word "bless" in our holy conversations it is if as something a Christian does not have, but must acquire and it is usually focused on a person's flesh. We will use the words "increase," "exceedingly" and "abundantly" to describe our blessings. This sounds very good to the average person. We read passages like (Deuteronomy 28:1-14). There you will read God saying you will be blessed in the city and in the country. Your offspring and your kneading bowl will be blessed. You will be blessed, coming and going. Your enemies will be defeated. The people of the world will be afraid of you. You will abound in prosperity. The work of your hands will be blessed. You will be the head and not the tail. This sounds incredible. But, as I said earlier, these are blessings of the flesh that we don't yet have and the only way to receive these blessings is also listed. *"All these blessings will come upon you and over-take you if you obey the Lord your God."* – Deuteronomy 28:2. God will bless you, *"If you keep the commandments of the Lord your God and walk in His ways."* – Deuteronomy 28:9. All of these blessings will be yours, *"If you listen to the commandments of the Lord your God, which I charge you today, to observe them carefully, and do not turn aside from any of the words which I command you today."* – Deuteronomy

28:13–14. All God desires from you in order to receive all of these blessings is your complete and total, 100 percent obedience to all that He commands. Prayerfully, we will soon learn that the true meaning of being "blessed" is having Jesus Christ.

If you have accepted Jesus Christ as your savior then you already have every spiritual blessing. Therefore, if you are looking for blessings of the flesh, you are missing out on what the Lord has freely given you in favor of trying to get something less satisfying and impossible to attain. Two of the spiritual blessings you have are that God, *"has reconciled you by Christ's physical body through death to present you holy in His sight, without blemish and free from accusation"* – Colossians 1:22, and you *"have been sanctified through the offering of the body of Jesus once for all."* – Hebrews 10:10. Just like the definition of blessed mentioned, you are holy and consecrated simply by your faith in Jesus Christ. This has been given to you as an inheritance of your faith not as a reward for your obedience. There are consequences to disobedience as stated in the rest of the chapter. God wants you to be enthusiastic about your life. What you truly need is already been given. You don't need a full "basket," you need a full "spirit." That only comes by faith.

Books of the Bible – Old Testament

The Old Testament (also known as the Jewish Tanakh) is the first 39 books in most Christian Bibles. The name stands for the original promise with God (to the descendants of Abraham in particular) prior to the coming of Jesus Christ in the New Testament (of the new promise). The Old Testament contains the creation of the universe, the history of the patriarchs, the exodus from Egypt, the formation as a nation, the subsequent decline and fall of the nation, the Prophets (who speak for God), and the Wisdom Books.

Genesis
Speaks of beginnings and is the foundation to the understanding of the rest of the Bible. It is supremely a book that speaks about relationships, highlighting those between God and his creation, between God and humankind, and between human beings.

Exodus
Describes the history of the Israelites leaving Egypt after slavery. The book lays a foundational theology in which God reveals his name, his attributes, his redemption, his law and how he is to be worshiped.

Leviticus
Receives its name from Septugiant (the pre-Christian Greek translation of the Old Testament) and means "concerning the Levities" (the priests of Israel). It serves as a manual of regulations enabling the holy King to set up hi early throne among the people

of his kingdom. It explains how they are to be holy people and to worship him in a holy manner.

Numbers
Numbers relates to the history of Israel's journey from Mount Sinai to the plains of Moab on the border of Canaan. The book tells of the murmuring and rebellion of God's people and of their subsequent judgment.

Deuteronomy
Deuteronomy ("repetition of the Law") serves as a reminder to God's people about His covenant. The book is "pause" before Joshua's conquest begins and a reminder of what God required.

Joshua
Joshua is a story of conquest and fulfillment for the people of God. After many years of slavery in Egypt and 40 years in the desert, the Israelites were finally allowed to enter the land promised to their fathers.

Judges
The book of Judges depicts the life of Israel in the Promised Land – from the death of Joshua to the rise of the monarchy. It tells of urgent appeals to God in times of crisis and apostasy, moving the Lord to raise up leaders (judges) through whom He throws off foreign oppressors and restores the land to peace.

Ruth
The book of Ruth has been called one of the best examples of short narrative ever written. It presents an account of the remnant of true and piety in the period of the judges through the fall and restoration of Naomi and her daughter-in-law Ruth (an ancestor of King David and Jesus).

1 Samuel
Samuel relates God's establishment of a political system in Israel headed by a human king. Through Samuel's life, we see the rise of the monarchy and the tragedy of its first king, Saul.

2 Samuel
After the failure of King Saul, 2 Samuel depicts David as a true (though imperfect) representative of the ideal theocratic king. Under David's rule the Lord caused the nation to prosper, to defeat its enemies, and to realize the fulfillment of His promises.

1 Kings
1 Kings continues the account of the monarchy in Israel and God's involvement through the prophets. After David, his son Solomon ascends the throne of a united kingdom, but this unity only lasts during his reign. The book explores how each subsequent king in Israel and Judah answers God's call – or, as often happens, fails to listen.

2 Kings
Carries the historical account of Judah and Israel forward. The kings of each nation are judged in light of their disobedience to the covenant with God. Ultimately, the people of both nations are exiled for disobedience.

1 Chronicles
Just as the author of Kings had organized and interpreted Israel's history to address the needs of the exiled community, so the writer of 1 Chronicles wrote for the restored community another history.

2 Chronicles
Continues the account of Israel's history with an eye for restoration of those who had returned from exile.

Ezra
The book of Ezra relates how God's covenant people were restored from Babylonian exile to the covenant land as a theocratic (kingdom of God) community even while continuing under the foreign rule.

Nehemiah
Closely related to the book of Ezra, Nehemiah chronicles the return of this "cupbearer to the king" and the challenges he and other Israelites face in their restored homeland.

Esther

Esther records the institution of the annual festive of Purim through the historical account of Esther, a Jewish girl who becomes of Persia and saves her people from destruction.

Job

Through a series of monologues, the book of Job relates the account of a righteous man who suffers under terrible circumstances. The book's profound insights, its literary structures, and the quality of its rhetoric display the author's genius.

Psalms

The Psalms are collected songs and poems that represent centuries worth of praises and prayers to God on a number of themes and circumstances. The Psalms are impassioned, vivid and concrete; they are rich in images, in simile and metaphor.

Proverbs

Proverbs was written to give "prudence to the simple, knowledge and discretion to the young," and to make the wise even wiser. The frequent references to "my son(s)" emphasize in instructing the young and guiding them in a way of life that yields rewarding results.

Ecclesiates

The author of Ecclesiastes puts his power of wisdom to work to examine the human experience and assess the human situation. His perspective is limited to what happens "under the sun" (as is that all human teachers).

Song of Solomon

In ancient Israel everything human came to expression in words: reverence, gratitude, anger, sorrow, suffering, trust, friendship, commitment. In the Song of Solomon, it is love that finds words – inspired words that disclose its exquisite charm and beauty as one of God's choicest gifts.

Isaiah

Isaiah son Amoz is often thought of as the greatest of the writing prophets. His name means. "The Lord saves." Isaiah is a book that unveils the full dimensions of God's judgment and salvation.

Jeremiah

This book preserves an account of the prophetic ministry of Jeremiah, whose personal life and struggles are shown to us in greater depth and detail than those of any other Old Testament prophet.

Lamentations

Lamentation consists of a series of poetic and powerful laments over the destruction of Jerusalem (the royal city of the Lord's kingdom) in 586 B.C.

Ezekiel

The Old Testament in general and the prophets in particular presuppose and teach a God's sovereignty over all creation and the course of history. And nowhere in the Bible are God's initiative and control expressed more clearly and pervasively than in the book of the prophet of Ezekiel.

Daniel

Daniel captures the major events in the life of the prophet Daniel during Israel's exile. His life and visions point to God's plans of redemption and sovereign control of history.

Hosea

The prophet Hosea son of Beeri lived in the tragic final days of the northern kingdom. His life served as a parable of God's faithfulness to an unfaithful Israel.

Joel

The prophet Joel warned the people of Judah about God's coming judgment – and the coming restoration and blessing that will come through repentance.

Amos

Amos prophesied during the reigns of Uzziah over Judah (79-730 B.C) and Jeroboam II over Israel 793-753).

Obadiah

The prophet Obadiah warned the proud people of Edom about the impending judgment coming upon them.

Jonah

Jonah is unusual as a prophetic book, in that it is a narrative account of Jonah's mission to the city of Nineveh, his resistance, his imprisonment in a great fish, his visit to the city, and the subsequent outcome.

Micah

Micah prophesied sometime between 50 and 686 B.C. during the reigns of Jothan, Ahaz, and Hezekiah, kings of Judah. Israel was in an apostate condition. Micah predicted the fall of her capital, Samaria, and also foretold the inevitable desolation of Judah.

Nahum

The book contains the "vision of Nahum," whose names means "comfort." The focal point of the entire book is the Lord's judgment on Nineveh for her oppression, cruelty, idolatry, and wickedness.

Habakkuk

Little is known about Habakkuk except that he was a contemporary of Jeremiah and a man of vigorous faith. The book bearing his name contains a dialogue between the prophet and God concerning injustice and suffering.

Zephaniah

The prophet Zephaniah was evidently a person of considerable social standing in Judah and was probably related to the royal line. The intent of the author was to announce to Judah God's approaching judgment.

Haggai

Haggai was a prophet who, along with Zechariah, encouraged the returned exiles to rebuild the temple. His prophecies clearly show the consequences of disobedience. When the people give priority to God and his house, they are blessed.

Zechariah

Like Jeremiah and Ezekiel, Zechariah was not only a prophet, but also a member of a priestly family. The chief purpose of Zechariah (and Haggai was to rebuke the people of Judah and to encourage and motivate them to complete the rebuilding of the temple.)

Malachi

Malachi, whose name means "my messenger," spoke to the Israelites after their return from exile. The theological message of the book can be summed up in one sentence. The Great King will come not only to judge his people, but also to bless and restore them.

The Ten Commandments

The Ten Commandments are listed twice in the Hebrew Bible, first at Exodus 20:1–17, and then at Deuteronomy 5:4–21. Both versions state that God inscribed them on two stone tablets, which he gave to Moses. According to New Testament writers, The Ten Commandments are clearly attributed to Moses (Mark 7:10).

And God spoke all these words: "I am the Lord, your God, who brought you out of Egypt, out of the land of slavery.

You shall have no other gods before me.

You shall not make for yourself an image in the form of anything in heaven above or on the earth beneath or in the waters below.

You shall not bow down to them or worship them; for I, the Lord your God, am a jealous God, punishing the children for the sin of the parents to the third and fourth generation of those who hate me, but showing love to a thousand generations of those who love me and keep my commandments.

You shall not misuse the name of the Lord your God, for the Lord will not hold anyone guiltless who misuses his name.

Remember the Sabbath day by keeping it holy. Six days you shall labor and do all your work, but the seventh day is a Sabbath to the Lord your God. On it you shall not do any work, neither you, nor your son or daughter, nor your male or female servant, nor your animal, nor any foreigner residing in your towns. For in six days the Lord made the heavens and the earth, the sea, and all that is in them, but he rested on the seventh day. Therefore the Lord blessed the Sabbath day and made it holy.

Honor your father and your mother, so that you may live long in the land the Lord your God is giving you.

You shall not murder.

You shall not commit adultery.

You shall not steal.

You shall not give false testimony against your neighbor.

You shall not covet your neighbor's house.

You shall not covet your neighbor's wife, or his male or female servant, his ox or donkey, or anything that belongs to your neighbor."

Who Were the 12 Disciples?

The 12 disciples/apostles of Jesus were the foundation stones of His church, several even wrote portions of the Bible. In Revelation 21:14 we are told that the twelve foundations of the wall of New Jerusalem will have in them the names of the twelve disciples/apostles. It is evident that God had great respect for these twelve men.

Andrew:
Andrew was the brother of Peter, and a son of Jonas. He lived in Bethsaida and Capernaum and was a fisherman before Jesus called him. Originally, he was a disciple of John the Baptist (Mark 1:16–18). Andrew brought his brother, Peter, to Jesus (John 1:40). He is the first to have the title of Home and Foreign Missionary. Andrew introduced others to Jesus. Although circumstances placed him in a position where it would have been easy for him to become jealous and resentful, he was optimistic and well content in second place. His main purpose in life was to bright others to the master. He was crucified on the X-shaped cross, which is still called Saint Andrew's cross and which is one of his apostolic symbols.

Bartholomew or Nathanael:
Bartholomew Nathanael, son of Talmai, lived in Cana of Galilee. His apostolic symbol is three parallel knives. Tradition says he was a missionary in Armenia. A number of scholars believe that he was the only one of the 12 disciples who came from royal blood, or noble birth. His name means Son of Tolmai or Talmai (2 Samuel 3:3). Talmai was king of Geshur whose daughter, Maacah, was the wife of David, mother of Absolom. He was a great searcher of the

Scripture and a scholar in the law and the prophets. He developed into a man of complete surrender to the Carpenter of Nazareth, and one of the Church's most adventurous missionaries. He died a martyr for his Lord. He was flayed alive with knives.

James the Elder:
He was a member of the Inner Circle, so called because they were accorded special privileges. The New Testament tells us very little about James. His name never appears apart from that of his brother, John. They were an inseparable pair. He was a man of courage and forgiveness, a man without jealousy, living in the shadow of John, a man of extraordinary faith. He was the first of the twelve to become a martyr. His symbol is three shells, the sign of his pilgrimage by the sea.

James the Lesser or the Younger:
James, the Lesser or Younger, son of Alpheus, or Cleophas and Mary, lived in Galilee. He was the brother of the Apostle Jude. According to tradition he wrote the Epistle of James, preached in Palestine and Egypt and was crucified in Egypt. James was one of the little-known disciples. Some scholars believe he was the brother of Matthew, the tax collector. James was a man of strong character and one of the most fiery type. Tradition tells us he also died as a martyr and his body was sawed in pieces. The saw became his apostolic symbol.

John:
John Boanerges, son of Zebedee and Salome, brother of James, the Apostle. He was known as the Beloved Disciple. A fisherman who lived in Bethsaida, Capernaum and Jerusalem, he was a member of the Inner Circle. He wrote the Gospel of John, I John, II John, III John, and Revelation. He preached among the churches of Asia Minor. He was banished to the isle of Patmos. He was a man of ambition and a man with an explosive temper and an intolerant heart. His second name Boanerges, which means son of Thunder. He and his brother, James, came from a more well-to-do family than the rest of the 12 Apostles. Since his father had hired servants in his fishing business (Mark 1:20) he may have felt himself above

the rest. He was close to Peter and they acted together in the ministry. It is said an attempt was made on his life by giving him a chalice of poison from which God spared his life. He died of natural causes. A chalice with a snake in it is his apostolic symbol.

Judas:
Judas Iscariot, the traitor, was the son of Simon who lived in Kerioth of Judah. He was the only disciples from Judah, all the others were from Galilee. He was the treasurer of the band and among the outspoken leaders. It is hard to believe that he could betray Jesus after being a witness to his many miracles and sitting under his teachings. Yet, he turned him over to the enemies by betraying him for thirty pieces of silver and afterwards hanged himself (Matthew 26:14, 16). His apostolic symbol is a hangman's noose, or a money purse with pieces of silver falling from it.

Jude of Thaddeus
Jude, Thaddeus, or Lebbeus, son of Alpheus or Cleophas and Mary. He was a brother of James the Younger. He was one of the very little-known Apostles and lived in Galilee. He wanted Jesus to be presented to the world. He asked Jesus at the Last Supper, "But Lord, why do you intend to show yourself to us and not to the world?" He wanted the Saviour to be shown to the world not as a suffering Saviour, but as a ruling King. He preached the gospel in Edessa near the Euphrates River. There many souls were saved and many people were healed. He was killed with arrows at Ararat. The chosen symbol for him is the ship because he was a missionary thought to be a fisherman.

Matthew or Levi:
Matthew or Levi, son of Alpheus, lived in Capernaum. He was a publican or tax collector. He wrote the Gospel that bears his name. Matthew name means a "gift of God." The name Levi could have been given to him by Jesus. It is likely that James the lesser, who was one of the twelve Apostles, was Matthew's brother, also son of Alpheus. Tax collectors had been known to assess duty payable at impossible sums and then offer to lend the money to travelers at a high rate of interest. Yet, Jesus chose a man all men hated and

made him one of His men. It took Jesus Christ to see the potential in the tax collector of Capernaum.

Matthew was unlike the other twelve Apostles, who were all fishermen. He could use a pen, and by his pen he became the first man to present to the world, in the Hebrew language, an account of the teaching of Jesus. He was the first man to write down the teachings of Jesus. He was a missionary of the Gospel, who laid down his life for the faith of his Master. The apostolic symbol of Matthew is three money bags which reminds us that he was a tax collector before Jesus called him. He died a martyr in Ethiopia.

Simon Peter:
Simon Peter, son of Jonas, was a fisherman who lived in Bethsaida and Capernaum. He did evangelistic work and missionary work among the Jews, going as far as Babylon. He was a member of the Inner Circle, and authored two New Testament epistles which bear his name.

Why Did God Give Us "Four" Gospels?

While the entire Bible is inspired by God (2 Timothy 3:16), He used human authors with different backgrounds and personalities to accomplish His purposes through their writing. Each of the gospel authors had a distinct purpose behind his gospel and in carrying out those purposes, each emphasized different aspects of the person and ministry of Jesus Christ.

Matthew was writing to a Hebrew audience, and one of his purposes was to show from Jesus' genealogy and fulfillment of Old Testament prophecies that He was the long-expected Messiah, and thus should be believed in. Matthew's emphasis is that Jesus is the promised King, the "Son of David," who would forever sit upon the throne of Israel (Matthew 9:27–29).

Mark, a cousin of Barnabas (Colossians 4:10), as an eyewitness to the events in the life of Christ as well as being a friend of the Apostle Peter. Mark wrote for a Gentile audience, as is brought out by not including things important to Jewish readers (genealogies, Christ's controversies with Jewish leaders of His day, frequent references to the Old Testament, etc.). Mark emphasizes Christ as the suffering Servant, the One who came not to be served, but to serve and give His life a ransom for many (Mark 10:45).

Luke, the "beloved physician" (Colossians 4:14 KJV), evangelist, and companion of the Apostle Paul, wrote both the gospel of Luke and the Acts of the apostles. Luke is the only Gentile author of the New Testament. He has long been accepted as a diligent master historian by those who have used his writings in genealogical and historical studies. Luke often refers to Christ as the "Son of Man," emphasizing His humanity, and he shares many details that are not found in the other gospel accounts.

John was an Apostle and is distinct from the other three Gospels and contains much theological content in regards to the person of Christ and the meaning of faith. Matthew, Mark and Luke are referred to as the "Synoptic Gospels" because of their similar styles and content and because they give a synopsis of the life of Christ. The gospel of John begins not with Jesus' birth or earthly ministry but with the activity and characteristics of the Son of God before He became man (John 1:14). The Gospel of John emphasizes the deity of Christ, as is seen in his use of such phrases as *"the Word was God"* (John 1:1), *"the Savior of the World"* (John 4:42), the *"Son of God"* (used repeatedly), and the *"Lord and…God"* (John 20:28). John is filled with Jesus affirming his deity with several of the "I AM" statements... "before Abraham was, I Am." John also emphasizes the fact that Jesus' humanity, desiring to show the error of a religious sect of his day, the Gnostics, who did not believe in Christ's humanity. John's gospel spells out his overall purpose for writing: *"Jesus did many other miraculous signs in the presence of his disciples, which are not recorded in this book. But these are written that you may believe that Jesus is the Christ, the Son of God, and that by believing you may have life in his name."* – John 20:30–31.

Little

Little: small amount of.

"Ho, every one that thirsteth, come ye to the waters, and he that hath no money; come and eat. Yea, come buy wine and milk without money, and without price. – Isaiah 55:1 (KJV)

Little is much when God is in it. In the midst of the Lord's ministry there was a problem – multitudes of people were in a desert place one late afternoon, and everyone was hungry. The disciples had 5,000 hungry men (John 6:10) on their hands. The Gospel of Matthew does not include women and children, so the total could be as much as 10,000 – 15,000. And yet what the Lord used to feed the multitudes was five loaves and two fishes (John 6: 9-10) with 12 baskets more to spare! The miracle of the feeding of the five thousand is the one miracle along with the resurrection that is included in all four Gospels. It held strong appeal, especially for those who had learned of Israel's experience in the wilderness when God "rained down manna upon them to eat, and give them food from heaven." God has always been a provider of His people's needs. He will always be.

When Jesus asked Philip where they could buy a great amount of bread, Philip started assessing the probable cost. He was the logical thinker of the group, the dollars and cents man. His reply stresses the hopelessness of the situation judged from the meager resources of the group. Two hundred denaril or eight months wages would not buy enough to give this crowd a little taste. Philip does not come up with a solution, but points out the hopeless impossibility. Jesus wanted to teach him that fmancial resources are not the most important ones. We can limit what God does in us by assuming what is and is not possible. Is there some impossible task that you believe God wants you to do? Don't let your estimate of what can't be done, keep you from taking on the task. God can do the miraculous; trust Him to provide the resources.

Andrew came to Jesus with a lad who had five barley loaves and two fish, but what are these for so many people? This child had volunteered his lunch, knowing it was not much but at least it was something. The lad brought that little he had, and it made a difference. If we offer nothing to God, He will have nothing to use. But only God can take what little we have and turn it into something great!

LITTLE IS MUCH WHEN GOD IS IN IT.

> A little bread becomes plenty.
> A little army becomes mighty.
> A little prayer gets answered.
> A little light becomes the universe.
> A little faith can move a mountain!

Yes! LITTLE IS MUCH WHEN GOD IS IN IT.

> This little light of mine
> I'm gonna let it shine.
> Let it Shine! Let it Shine! Let it Shine!

Baptism or Invitation to Discipleship

The proclamation of God's Word calls for our faithful response. After the sermon, the people may be called to discipleship, giving opportunity for any who wish to make or renew personal commitment to Christ and his realm. These words are appropriately delivered by an elder from the baptismal font.

All who thirst, come to the waters. – Jesus said: *"Those who drink of the water that I give will never be thirsty. The water that I give will be a spring for them, gushing up to eternal life."* – Isaiah 55:1, John 4:14.

Baptism is the way we become members of the church, the body of Christ or family of God. It is a sign of everything God has promised us: new life in Jesus, forgiveness of sin, and the coming of a new creation. When Jesus was baptized, the Holy Spirit rested on him like a bird from heaven, and God said, *"You are my beloved child."* God says the same thing to us when we are baptized.

Everyone who is baptized is a kind of minister – called to live like Jesus, to love others, and to serve God. Each one of us is given special gifts from the Holy Spirit to help us do these things. When we remember our baptism, we give thanks for these gifts and this calling, and we promise again to follow Jesus in everything we do.

Think of it as the ABCs.

ADMIT – you are a sinner. *"For all have sinned and come short of the glory of God."* – Romans 3:23. We can never be good enough on our own to deserve salvation because all of us have sinned; therefore we are guilty as charged.

BELIEVE – that Jesus is God's son and accept God's gift of forgiveness from sin. *"For God so loved the world he gave his only begotten son that whosoever believeth in him shall not perish but have everlasting life."* – John 3:16.

CONFESS – your faith in Jesus Christ as Savior and Lord. If you declare with your mouth, "Jesus is Lord," and believe in your heart that God raised him from the dead, you will be saved. (Romans 10:9)

Prayer of Salvation

Lord, I have sinned and come short of your glory. I know I need a Savior. Jesus, I believe you are God's Son. I believe that you were born of the Virgin Mary, that you lived on this earth, that you were crucified, that you died on Calvary and that you were buried. I believe that when you paid the penalty for my sin and for the sin of the whole world. Jesus, I believe that you did not stay dead, but that you got up from that grave with all power in your hands. I believe that you went back to heaven and that right now you are seated at the right hand of God Almighty. And I believe you are coming back again to get all of those who believe in you. Lord, I want to ask you to come into my heart right now. I turn away from my sins. I want you to be my Savior and Lord. And I believe that by praying this prayer and asking you to come into my life, that you are doing so and that I am saved right now. Lord, thank you for saving me!

The Eight Beatitudes of Jesus

Jesus gave us the eight Beatitudes in the Sermon on the Mount, recorded for all posterity in the Gospel of Matthew, the first Book of the New Testament of the Bible. Matthew's gospel was directed to an audience steeped in Hebrew tradition. The gospel stressed that Jesus is the Christ or Messiah foretold in Hebrew Scripture, our Old Testament, and that the Kingdom of the Lord is the Kingdom of God in Heaven. Jesus offers us a way of life that promises eternity in the Kingdom of Heaven.

"Blessed are the poor in spirit, for theirs is the kingdom of heaven." Poor in spirit means to be humble. Humility is the realization that all your gifts and blessings come from the grace of God. To have poverty of spirit means to be completely empty and open to the Word of God. Humility brings an openness and an inner peace, allowing one to do the will of God.

"Blessed are they who mourn, for they shall be comforted." Mourning in this context is called a blessing, because mourning our fallen nature creates in us a desire to improve ourselves and to do the right thing. We are made in the image and likeness of God and lived in Paradise, in the Garden of Eden, and compared to our present state after the Fall, one can only mourn our present condition. But God says we would be "comforted" by the Comforter, the Holy Spirit, and hopefully one day in the Kingdom of Heaven.

"Blessed are the meek, for they shall inherit the earth." The Beatitudes build one upon another. A humble person becomes meek, or becomes gentle kind, and exhibits docility of spirit, even in the face of adversity and hardship. A meek person exhibits self-control. Obedience is meekness toward our God.

"Blessed are they who hunger and thirst for righteousness, for they shall be satisfied." Justice and righteousness in the New Covenant indicate the fulfillment of God's will in your heart and soul. It is not mere observation of the law (Matthew 5:20), but rather an expression of brotherly love. A continuous desire for justice and moral perfection will lead on to a fulfillment of that desire – a transition and conversion to holiness.

"Blessed are the merciful, for they shall obtain mercy." Mercy is the loving disposition towards those who suffer distress. Love, compassion, and forgiveness towards one's neighbor will bring peace in your relationships. Jesus reminds us that whatever *"you did to the least of my brethren, you did it to me."* – Matthew 25:31–46.

"Blessed are the pure of heart, for they shall see God." To be pure of heart means to be free of all selfish intentions and self-seeking desires. What a beautiful goal to work toward in our lives!! How many of us have performed an act perfectly free of any personal gain? Such an act is pure love. This brings happiness to your soul.

"Blessed are the peacemakers, for they shall be called the children of God." Jesus gives us peace – *"Peace I leave with you; My peace I give to you."* – John 14:27. Peace is also a fruit of the Spirit (Galatians 5:22). Peacemakers not only live peaceful lives but also try to bring peace and friendship to others, and to preserve peace between God and man. But one cannot give another what one does not possess oneself. The Lord wants you to be filled with peace yourself, and then to pass it on to others.

"Blessed are they who are persecuted for the sake of the righteousness, for theirs is the kingdom of heaven." – Matthew 5:3–10. Jesus said many times that those who follow him will be persecuted. *"Blessed are you when men revile you and persecute you and utter all kinds of evil against you falsely on my account. Rejoice and be glad, for your reward is great in heaven, for so men persecuted the prophets who were before you."* – Matthew 5:11–12. Stephen, Peter and Paul, nearly all of the Apostles, and many Christians in the Roman era suffered martyrdom. Oppressive governments and endless conflicts in the last one hundred years, such as World Wars I and II, and the Middle East wars in Iraq, Egypt, and Syria have seen their share of martyrs.

But the Lord promised those that suffer for his sake will be rewarded with the Kingdom of Heaven!

Books of the Bible – New Testament

The New Testament is a collection of 27 books, usually placed after the Old Testament in most Christian Bibles. The name refers to the new covenant (or promise) between God and humanity through the death and resurrection of Jesus Christ. The New Testament chronicles the life and ministry of Jesus, the growth and impact of the early church, and instructive letters to early churches.

Matthew
Matthew's main purpose in writing his Gospel (the "good news") is to prove to his Jewish readers that Jesus is their Messiah. He does this primarily by showing how Jesus in his life and ministry fulfilled the Old Testament Scriptures.

Mark
Since Mark's Gospel (the "good news") is traditionally associated with Rome, it may have been occasioned by the persecutions of the Roman church in the period c. A.D. 64-67. Mark may be writing to prepare his readers for such suffering by placing before them the life of our Lord.

Luke
Luke's Gospel (the "good news") was written to strengthen the faith of all believers and to answer the attacks of unbelievers. It was presented to debunk some disconnected and ill-founded reports about Jesus. Luke wanted to show that the place of the Gentile (non-Jewish) Christian in God's kingdom is based on the teaching of Jesus.

John

John's Gospel (the "good news") is rather different from the other three, highlighting events not detailed in the others. The author himself sates his main purpose clearly in 20:31: *"that you may believe that Jesus is the Christ, the Son of God, and that by believing you may have life in his name."*

Acts

The book of Acts provides a bridge from the writings of the New Testament. As a second volume to Luke's Gospel, it joins what Jesus "began to do and to teach" as told in the Gospels with what he continued to do and teach through the apostles' preaching and the establishment of the church.

Romans

Paul's primary theme in Romans is presenting the gospel (the "good news"), God's plan of salvation and righteousness for all humankind, Jew and non-Jew alike.

I Corinthians

The first letter to the Corinthians revolves around the theme of problems in Christian conduct in the church. It thus has to do with progressive sanctification, the continuing development of a holy character. Obviously Paul was personally concerned with the Corinthian's problems, revealing a true pastor's (shepherd's) heart.

2 Corinthians

Because of the occasion that prompted this letter, Paul had a number of purposes in mind: to express the comfort and joy Paul felt because the Corinthians had responded favorably to his painful letter; to let them know about the trouble he went through in the province of Asia; and to explain to them the true nature (its joys, sufferings and rewards) and high calling of Christian ministry.

Galatians

Galatians stands as an eloquent and vigorous apologetic for the essential New Testament truth that people are justified by faith in Jesus Christ – by nothing less and nothing more – and that they are sanctified not by legalistic works but by the obedience that comes from faith in God's work for them.

Ephesians
Unlike several of the other letters Paul wrote, Ephesians does not address any particular error or heresy. Paul wrote to expand the horizons of his readers, so that they might understand better the dimensions of God's eternal purpose and grace and come to appreciate the high goals God has for the church.

Philippians
Paul's primary purpose in writing this letter was to thank the Philippians for the gift they had sent him upon learning of his detention at Rome. However, he makes use of this occasion to fulfill several other desires: 1. To report on his own circumstances; 2. to encourage the Philippians to stand firm in the face of persecution and rejoice regardless of circumstances; and 3. to exhort them to humility and unity.

Colossians
Paul's purpose is to refute the Colossian heresy. To accomplish this goal, he exalts Christ at the very image of God, the Creator, the preexistent sustainer of all things, the head of the church, the first to be resurrected, the fullness of deity (god) in bodily form, and the reconciler.

1 Thessalonians
Although the thrust of the letter is varied, the subject of eschatology (doctrine of last things) seems to be predominant in both Thessalonian letters. Every chapter of 1 Thessalonians ends with a reference to the second coming of Christ.

2 Thessalonians
Although the thrust of the letter is varied, the subject of eschatology (doctrine of last things) seems to be predominant in both Thessalonian letters. Every chapter of 1 Thessalonians ends with a reference to the second coming of Christ.

1 Timothy

During his fourth missionary journey, Paul had instructed Timothy to care for the church at Ephesus while he went on to Macedonia. When he realized that he might not return to Ephesus in the near future, he wrote "Pastoral Epistles."

2 Timothy

Paul was concerned about the welfare of the churches during this time of persecution under Nero, and he admonishes Timothy to guard the gospel, to persevere in it, to keep on preaching it, and, if necessary, to suffer for it. This is the second "Pastoral Epistle."

Titus

Apparently Paul introduced Christianity in Crete when he and Titus visited the island, after which he left Titus there to organize the converts. Paul sent with Zenas and Apollos, who were on a journey that took them through Crete, to give Titus personal authorization and guidance in meeting opposition, instructions about faith and conduct, and warnings about false teachers. This is the last of the "Pastoral Epistles."

Philemon

To win Philemon's willing acceptance of the runaway slave Onesimus, Paul writes very tactfully and in a lighthearted tone, which he creates with wordplay. The appeal is organized in a way prescribed by ancient Greek and Roman teachers: to build rapport, to persuade the mind, and to move the emotions.

Hebrews

The theme of Hebrews is the absolute supremacy and sufficiency of Jesus Christ as revealer and as mediator of God's grace. A striking feature of this presentation of the gospel is the unique manner in which the author employs expositions of eight specific passages of the Old Testament Scriptures.

James

Characteristics that make the letter distinctive are: 1. Its unmistakably Jewish nature; 2. Its emphasis on vital Christianity, characterized by good deeds and a faith that works (genuine faith must and will be accompanied by a consistent lifestyle); 3. Its simple organization; 4. and its familiarity with Jesus' teachings preserved in the Sermon on the Mount.

1 Peter
Although 1 Peter is a short letter, it touches on various doctrines and has much to say about Christian life and duties. It is not surprising that different readers have found it to have different principal themes. For example, it has been characterized as a letter of separation, of suffering and persecution, of suffering and glory, of hope, of pilgrimage, of courage, and as a letter dealing with the true grace of God.

2 Peter
In his first letter Peter feeds Christ's sheep by instructing them how to deal with persecution from outside the church; in this second letter he teaches them how to deal with false teachers and evildoers who have come into the church.

1 John
John's readers were confronted with an early form of Gnostic teaching of the Cerinthian variety. This heresy was also libertine, throwing off all moral restraints. Consequently, John wrote this letter with two basic purposes in mind: 1. to expose false teachers and 2. to give believers assurance of salvation.

2 John
During the first two centuries the gospel was taken from place to place by traveling evangelists and teachers. Believers customarily took these missionaries into their homes and gave then provisions for their journey when they left. Since Gnostic teachers also relied on this practice, 2 John was written to urge discernment in supporting traveling teachers.

3 John

Itinerant teachers sent out by John were rejected in one of the churches in the province of Asia by a dictatorial leader, Diotrephes, who even excommunicated members who showed hospitality to John's messengers. John wrote this letter to commend Gaius for supporting the teachers and, indirectly, to warn Diotrephes.

Jude

Although Jude as very eager to write to his readers about salvation, he felt that he must instead warn them about certain immoral men circulating among them who were perverting the grace of God. Apparently, these false teachers were trying to convince believers that being saved by grace gave them license to sins would no longer be held against them.

Revelation

John writes to encourage the faithful to resist staunchly the demands of emperor worship. He informs his readers that the final showdown between God and Satan will increase his persecution of believers, but they must stand fast, even to death. They are sealed against any spiritual harm and will soon be vindicated when Christ returns, when the wicked are forever destroyed, and when God's people enter an eternity of glory and blessedness.

The Significance of the Number "12"

Jesus chose twelve disciples to be with Him during the course of His ministry on earth, to see Him after His resurrection, and to lay the foundations of His Church; sent forth as missionaries by the church at Antioch. The twelve were: Simon who he called also Peter, Andrew, James and John, Philip, Bartholomew, Thomas, Matthew, James son of Alphaeus, Simon called the Zealot, Jude son of James, and Judas Iscariot, replaced after the Ascension by Matthias. (Luke 6, 12–16; Matthew 10, 2–4; Mark 3, 16–19; Acts 1, 13).

Twelve is a perfect number; signifying God's power and authority, as well as service as a perfect governmental foundation. It is found as a multiple in all that has to do with rule. Twelve the product of three (the perfectly Divine and heavenly number) and four (the earthly of what is material and organic).

> The Twelve Patriarchs
> The Twelve Sons of Israel
> The Twelve Apostles
> The Twelve foundations in the heavenly realm
> The Twelve Gates
> The Twelve Pearls
> The Twelve Angels
> The Twelve Stars
> The woman with the issue of blood suffered twelve years
> The twelve stones on the breastplates of high priests
> The twelve minor prophets in the Old Testament
> Jesus appeared in public at the age of twelve

New Jerusalem, which is made in heaven and brought to the earth by God himself, contains 12 gates made of pearl which are each manned by an angel. Over each gate will be one of the names of Israel's twelve tribes. The walls are 144 cubits high (12 multiplied by itself – Revelation 21:16–17), with the city itself being 12,000 furloughs square.

About Brenda Smith

When meeting Brenda C. Smith, for the first time, you will soon discover this overjoyed, full of life Christian woman "walks her talk."

"I've always loved to write. I started writing poetry at a very early age, and thought it was great the way I could make the words rhyme. I was hooked! Not only on the rhyming of the words, but having the ability to put in words what beauty I saw in nature and the experiences in my life," exclaims Brenda. Her mother encouraged her to write – pursuing the thing that makes you happy was your gift in life.

Brenda loves the Word of God and how it makes her feel loved, wanted and needed in this world. She grew up attending church back in the times when you went to church at 10:00 a.m. on a Sunday morning, and you came back home after the 6:00 p.m. night service. "We 'churched' all day, and I wouldn't have it any other way," remarks Brenda. Without the Gospel of Jesus Christ, Brenda whole-heartly believes that we would all be lost, and it is her duty as a Christian to help lift the spirit of those who are down-trodden.

After attending her first writer's workshop, Brenda left with the determination someday she would be a writer of Christian literature. Now, she writes articles for several Christian publications. "My God, my family and my work have provided a vast array of subject matter for my writing," says Brenda. She also conducts a ministry on Facebook called B.A.L.M. (Bereavement and Loss Ministry), helping others through the grieving process. Brenda's *Thursday's Word* blog is emailed weekly as an outreach to encourage people who are having struggles in life. This book is a collection of Biblical devotionals and poetry from her popular weekly blog, *Thursday's Word*. As you absorb Brenda Smith's devotionals and poetry, she will inspire you to "WALK YOUR TALK" in your daily Christian life.

Brenda attended Lipscomb University in Nashville, Tennessee, majoring in Business Administration and Biblical Ethics. She was awarded a Bachelor of Religious Education degree from Tennessee Bible College, Cookeville, Tennessee.

Brenda has three children: Quinton, Quinesha, and Quandre' and one grandson, Caneen, who is her "joy." She resides in historic Franklin, Tennessee.

ORDER COPIES OF THIS BOOK NOW!

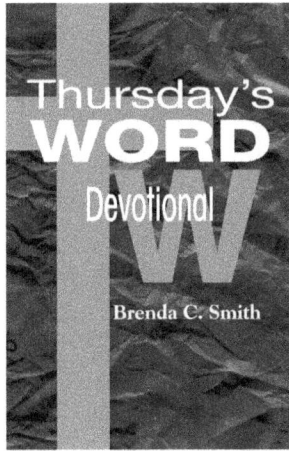

NO. OF COPIES___*Thursday's Word* @ $17.^{95} each ___x no. of copies

SUBTOTAL	_____
Add 9.25 % sales tax (Tenn.. residents only)	_____
Postage and handling for 1st book - $3.^{75}	_____
P & H for each additional book - $1.^{00}	_____
TOTAL	_____

ORDERED BY _____

STREET/APT NO. _____

CITY/STATE/ZIP_____

PHONE (_____)_____

Your email address: _____
We would like to send you product updates by email.

MAKE YOUR CHECK OR MONEY ORDER TO: BRENDA C. SMITH
PLEASE MAIL THIS ORDER FORM WITH YOUR PAYMENT TO:
Brenda C. Smith, P.O. Box 405, Franklin TN 37064
Please allow 2 weeks for delivery. Prices are subject to change without notice.

www.ingramcontent.com/pod-product-compliance
Lightning Source LLC
Chambersburg PA
CBHW050001100426
42739CB00011B/2465